C000213472

TURKEY

Recipes and tales from the road

TURKEY

Recipes and tales from the road

LEANNE KITCHEN

MURDOCH BOOKS

CONTENTS

INTRODUCTION

No matter how exhausted I am after the long flight from Sydney, I start to revive when I see the Istanbul skyline come into view, punctuated as it is by hundreds of minarets and framed by stretches of deep, blue water. There is simply nowhere else on earth quite like Turkey. By now I know Istanbul well enough to be able to make an instant beeline for my favourite shops, snack stops and restaurants, but I'm still a sucker for many of the city's more clichéd, if defining, charms, such as the müezzin, whose competing calls to prayer from the mosques of Sultanahmet bounce and echo around the ancient cobblestone streets like some sort of sonorous aria.

In common with most Islamic cultures, there's a particular kindness shown to strangers travelling in Turkey. In large and very touristy places like central Istanbul this kindness is not so apparent; although the endless cups of tea offered by those trying to flog something (often a carpet) could be construed as hospitality, albeit with a distinctly commercial edge. The further off the tourist track I go, the greater the chance I'll be invited to join someone for a snack, or even a home-cooked meal. The tradition of Turkish hospitality forms the perfect framework within which to enjoy the other major reason I so love to come here — the food. Journeying to Turkey, for me, is as much about meeting people and understanding the culture as it is about sharing meals and tasting new flavours.

Every time I disappear into some urban labyrinth or down an isolated village path with a new 'friend' I marvel at my willingness to go. After all, that young girl inviting me home for tea could be a kleptomaniac, hell-bent on stealing my credit cards. Those picnicking Kurds are no doubt eyeing me up with white slavery in mind (if you never hear from me again it's because I'm feeding horses, ploughing dirt and hunting with falcons, utterly against my will, somewhere in deepest, darkest Hakkari province). Nothing like this has ever happened of course, but my point is this: I wouldn't be so keen to trot after someone I'd barely met, on the promise of being fed and filled with tea, back home. I'd be considered certifiable.

Turks are extremely proud of their culinary culture and rightly so; it's a rich, varied and venerable cuisine. It is borne of many influences and sources. There are the courtly Ottoman-derived dishes (vestiges of which survive in and around Istanbul and other major centres like Bursa), right through to humble Anatolian peasant fare that speaks of a persistent reliance on the land and the seasons. It produces foodstuffs, ancient in origin, such as yoghurts, cheeses and preserved meats, that derive from an earlier, nomadic lifestyle once prevalent throughout Asia Minor. Turkey shares its border with eight nations: Greece, Bulgaria, Georgia, Armenia, Azerbaijan, Iran, Iraq and Syria; all of these have exerted a culinary influence. Until relatively recently, there were significant Greek, Armenian and Jewish communities in the country and their culinary legacy is now so interwoven into the Turkish kitchen vernacular it is impossible to know where one influence ends and another begins.

Modern Turkish cookery is hardly homogenous. Within her borders are seven incredibly diverse regions and not only are these quite distinct culinarily, but within each of the regional borders lie towns, cities and villages which have their own unique dishes, produce and even cooking styles. In Tekirdağ, for example, a town on the Marmara Sea, they make a famous variant of the ubiquitous köfte that's unlike any other. In Edirne, near the border with Bulgaria and Greece, they serve a celebrated liver dish that folk will drive three hours from Istanbul just to eat. From the watermelons of Diyarbakir, the tulum cheese of Erzincan, Isparta rosewater, wheat flour from Konya, Van honey and baldo rice from Tosya to hazelnuts from Giresun, Turkey is a veritable larder of extraordinary produce. And it has a trove of regional dishes that put it to varied and delicious use.

To date, not an awful lot has been documented about regional Turkish cuisine, even within the country. Many Turks are oblivious to the rich culinary diversity on their own doorstep. Little wonder really, as specialities, such as some cheeses and preserves, are made in specific and often far-flung villages and don't get exported further than the nearest large town. Fresh ingredients specific to a region, particularly wild ones like the spring greens of the Aegean, can't readily be found anywhere else.

There are also constants in the general Turkish diet as any visitor to the place will know. Yoghurt, kebabs, börek, gözleme, lahmacun, pide and çorba are staples countrywide. In the west of Turkey, particularly in Istanbul, the service of meze is elevated to something of an art form with myriad varieties available. Because of the homogenous nature of much of Turkish restaurant food, and the fact that most of the really interesting stuff gets cooked in the home or on special occasions, digging beyond the standard offerings can be hard. Scoring an invite to eat a home-cooked dinner, or patronising a restaurant specialising in a specific regional cuisine, are often the only real chances to eat beyond the usual.

My travels through Turkey were fairly random and this is reflected in the recipe content of this book — a collection of some of the best dishes I documented during my travels. Many of these I had researched and sought out, venturing to towns that are well known for their culinary efforts, and others I was fortunate enough to stumble upon by coincidence. I never set out to write the definitive word on Turkish cuisine, but rather let myself be led by the hospitable people of the nation, who were kind enough to share the recipes herein.

MEZE

From a Persian word meaning 'pleasant taste', meze refers to a variety of small food items usually served before a main course. Around Istanbul and coastal parts of Turkey, seafood is the main feature, while along the Aegean shoreline, vibrantly flavoured local cheeses and wild greens are a favourite. Meze can be as simple as a few lumps of feta, some olives and sliced pastirma, or it can include more elaborate preparations such as stuffed, deep-fried calamari, filled filo pastries or vine leaf rolls stuffed with spice-scented rice. Serve enough meze and you've got an entire meal on your hands. Serve enough raki to go with them, turn up the *fasil* music and you've got a party.

SPICED RED LENTIL KÖFTE

Rinse the burghul under cold running water, then drain well and set aside.

Put the lentils and 500 ml (17 fl oz/2 cups) water in a saucepan over medium–low heat. Bring slowly to a simmer, cover, and cook for 15–20 minutes, or until very tender. Remove from the heat and stir in the burghul. Cover and stand for 15 minutes, or until the mixture is very thick.

Meanwhile, heat the olive oil in a small frying pan over medium–low heat. Add the onion and garlic and cook, stirring often, for 7–8 minutes, or until softened. Add the tomato paste, pepper paste, cumin and paprika and continue stirring for 2–3 minutes, or until fragrant. Stir into the lentil mixture until well combined, then re-cover the pan and set aside until cool.

Once cool, season the lentil mixture with sea salt and freshly ground black pepper. Mix in the lemon juice and chilli, using your hands to knead the mixture well and adding a little extra oil or water if the mixture is too dry.

Take 1 tablespoon of mixture at a time and roll into balls, then use your thumb or a finger to make a deep indentation in each. Arrange the köfte balls on a serving plate and drizzle with the extra oil. Serve with the lettuce leaves, spring onion and lemon wedges. **SERVES 6**

Note: Turkish pepper paste is a thick red paste made from chillies and salt. It is mainly used as a flavouring, and is available from Middle Eastern and Turkish grocery stores and some delicatessens .

125 g (4^1/$_2$ oz/^{3}/$_4$ cup) fine burghul (bulgur)

185 g (6^1/$_2$ oz/^{3}/$_4$ cup) red lentils

2^1/$_2$ tablespoons extra virgin olive oil, plus extra, for drizzling

1 large onion, peeled and finely chopped

2 garlic cloves, very finely chopped

1 tablespoon tomato paste (concentrated purée)

1^1/$_2$ tablespoons Turkish pepper paste (see note)

1^1/$_2$ teaspoons ground cumin

1^1/$_2$ teaspoons paprika

1 tablespoon freshly squeezed lemon juice

1 large pinch chilli powder

baby cos (romaine) lettuce leaves, to serve

4 spring onions (scallions), roots removed and trimmed, to serve

Turkish bread or flat bread (see page 63), to serve

lemon wedges, to serve

SMOKY EGGPLANT, CARROT AND CARAWAY, AND BEETROOT AND YOGHURT DIPS

INGREDIENTS

crisp lavash or flat bread (see page 63),
    to serve

SMOKY EGGPLANT DIP

1.2 kg (2 lb 10 oz/about 3) eggplants
    (aubergines)
80 ml (2½ fl oz/⅓ cup) extra virgin
    olive oil
2 garlic cloves, crushed
2½ tablespoons freshly squeezed lemon
    juice, or to taste
250 g (9 oz/1 cup) Greek-style yoghurt

CARROT AND CARAWAY DIP

2½ tablespoons extra virgin olive oil
700 g (1 lb 9 oz/about 4) carrots, grated
½ teaspoon caraway seeds
250 g (9 oz/1 cup) Greek-style yoghurt

BEETROOT AND YOGHURT DIP

650 g (1 lb 7 oz/about 3) beetroot (beets),
    trimmed
2½ tablespoons extra virgin olive oil,
    plus extra, for brushing
2 garlic cloves
250 g (9 oz/ 1 cup) Greek-style yoghurt

SMOKY EGGPLANT DIP

Place the eggplants directly over a low flame and cook for about 20 minutes, turning often, until the skin is blackened all over and the centres are soft. (Alternatively, cook the eggplants on a barbecue grill heated to high.) Transfer the eggplants to a large bowl and cool slightly. When cool enough to handle, peel off the skins, removing as much of the blackened skin as possible and trim the stem end. Transfer the flesh to a colander and drain for about 20 minutes to remove any excess liquid.

Transfer the eggplant to a large bowl and use a fork to mash well. Add the olive oil, garlic, lemon juice and yoghurt and stir well to combine. Season with sea salt and freshly ground black pepper. Serve at room temperature with bread. Store in an airtight container in the refrigerator for up to 2 days. **SERVES 6**

CARROT AND CARAWAY DIP

Heat the oil in a saucepan over medium–low heat. Add the carrot, cover, and cook for 20 minutes, stirring often, until the carrot is very tender. Remove from the heat and cool to room temperature. Add the caraway seeds and yoghurt, season with sea salt and freshly ground black pepper and stir well to combine. Serve immediately with Turkish bread or refrigerate until needed. Carrot and caraway dip can be stored in an airtight container in the refrigerator for up to 2 days. Bring it back to room temperature and stir well before serving. **SERVES 6**

BEETROOT AND YOGHURT DIP

Preheat the oven to 180°C (350°F/Gas 4). Brush each beetroot with a little olive oil to coat, then individually wrap them in foil and place in a small roasting tin. Roast the beetroot for 1 hour 40 minutes, or until tender. Remove from the oven and cool to room temperature.

Grate the beetroot into a large bowl or cut into 5 mm (¼ inch) cubes and combine with the olive oil, garlic and yoghurt, stirring well to combine; season with sea salt and freshly ground black pepper. Serve immediately with Turkish bread or refrigerate until needed. Beetroot and yoghurt dip can be stored in an airtight container in the refrigerator for up to 2 days. Bring it back to room temperature and stir well before serving. **SERVES 6**

At its very essence Turkish food is incredibly simple. While there are complex dishes in the country's culinary lexicon, it's dishes such as this one that stand out. A humble ingredient such as the leek is treated in such a way as to taste truly and deeply of itself.

LEEKS WITH LEMON, CURRANTS AND TULUM

METHOD

Preheat the oven to 180°C (350°F/Gas 4). For baby leeks, pull off any tough outer layers and trim 3–4 cm (1¼–1½ inches) from the tops. Trim the roots, taking care to leave the root ends intact or they will fall apart during cooking. For large leeks, trim and discard the green part of the leeks and any long roots, then cut in half lengthways. Soak the leeks in clean water, taking care to remove all the dirt trapped between the layers. Place in a single layer in a large roasting tin.

Heat the olive oil in a small saucepan over medium–low heat. Add the garlic and cook for 2 minutes, or until fragrant. Pour the oil mixture over the leeks in the tin. Scatter over the sugar, lemon zest and currants then pour over the lemon juice and stock; season with freshly ground black pepper. Cover the tin tightly with foil and bake for about 25 minutes for baby leeks, or 50 minutes for the large ones — the leeks will be tender when done. Remove from the oven, drain the leeks and set aside, reserving the cooking liquid.

Transfer the reserved cooking liquid to a saucepan over high heat and bring to the boil. Cook for 10 minutes, or until the liquid has reduced and thickened, then pour over the leeks. Season with sea salt and cool. Once cool, transfer to a serving dish, scatter over the crumbled tulum cheese and serve. **SERVES 4**

Note: Tulum cheese is a white, crumbly sheep's milk cheese that is traditionally aged in a 'bag' made from the hide of the animal. Strong and pleasantly sharp in flavour, you can find it if you are lucky enough to live near a Middle Eastern or Turkish grocery store. Feta is a fine substitute if tulum cheese is unavailable.

INGREDIENTS

750 g (1 lb 10 oz/2 bunches) baby leeks or
    4 large leeks

125 ml (4 fl oz/½ cup) extra virgin olive oil

2 garlic cloves, thinly sliced

2½ teaspoons caster (superfine) sugar

finely grated zest of 1 lemon

35 g (1¼ oz/¼ cup) currants

50 ml (1½ fl oz) freshly squeezed lemon juice

375 ml (13 fl oz/1½ cups) chicken stock

2 thyme sprigs

125 g (4½ oz) tulum cheese (see note),
    crumbled

The roots of this meze classic lie in Georgian cooking (walnuts are a big feature of that cuisine). In Turkey it's served doused in sauce, although I've lightened the effect here and added a few greens. Use the freshest walnuts you can find. This dish tastes even better the next day but bring it to room temperature before serving.

CHICKEN AND WALNUT SALAD

INGREDIENTS

1.5 kg (3 lb 5 oz) whole free-range chicken

1 carrot

1 onion

2 celery sticks

1 fresh bay leaf

1 teaspoon whole allspice berries

1 cinnamon stick

125 g (4½ oz) day-old rustic bread, crusts removed

3 garlic cloves, chopped

200 g (7 oz/2 cups) walnut halves

125 ml (4 fl oz/½ cup) olive oil

2½ teaspoons red wine vinegar, or to taste

125 g (4½ oz/½ cup) whole egg mayonnaise

1 teaspoon dried chilli flakes, or to taste, plus extra to serve

2½ teaspoons sweet paprika

3 spring onions (scallions), trimmed and cut into long strips

120 g (4¼ oz/4 cups) watercress sprigs

METHOD

Put the whole chicken into a large saucepan with the carrot, onion, celery, bay leaf, allspice and cinnamon stick and add just enough cold water to cover. Cover with a lid and bring to a gentle simmer over medium–low heat for 45 minutes — do not let the water boil or the chicken will be tough. When the chicken is tender, remove from the liquid and cool to room temperature. Strain the cooking liquid, discarding the solids. Skim any fat from the surface of the liquid and reserve. Remove the chicken flesh from the bones, discarding the skin and bones and breaking the flesh into coarse chunks. Set aside.

Soak the bread in water for 1–2 minutes, then use your hands to squeeze out as much water as possible. Combine in a food processor with the garlic, walnuts, olive oil and vinegar and process until a coarse paste forms. Add the mayonnaise, chilli flakes, paprika and 125 ml (4 fl oz/½ cup) of the reserved cooking liquid and process until the mixture is smooth, thick and creamy, adding a little more cooking liquid if needed. Season with sea salt and freshly ground black pepper and a little more vinegar, to taste.

Place the spring onion into a bowl of iced water and stand for 3–4 minutes, or until curled slightly, then drain well. Toss in a bowl with the watercress and divide between serving plates. Combine the chicken in a bowl with just enough of the walnut sauce to lightly coat. Pile on top of the watercress and sprinkle with extra chilli flakes, to taste. Serve immediately with the remaining sauce passed separately. **SERVES 4–6**

A MORNING IN ISTANBUL

It's tricky to narrow down my favourite food experience in a city as large and diverse as Istanbul, but if I had just one morning there, based on the many times I've visited, this is most likely how I'd spend it.

I'd breakfast in the same, no-frills place around the corner from the Hippodrome in Sultanahmet where I always go. It's nothing special, just a workers' canteen really, but I like the poğaça. Afterwards, I'd follow the light rail track past the old train station that is still in use and once the terminus for the fabled *Orient Express*. At the food market near the glorious Yeni Cami (or 'new' mosque), vendors arrive early to set up their shops with spices, cheese, vine leaves and pickles, nuts, pastirma and sujuk. It's a good place for a scratch-and-sniff foray — I'd taste tulum cheese from Erzurum, still in its goat-hide casing; minci, a salty cheese from Trabzon; the finest pastirma from Kayseri; and sweet jam from Kastamonu, famous for its wild strawberries. Even with a stomach lined with breakfast, I can never say no.

Next, I'd skip behind the spice bazaar to the warren of streets filled with copper and sweet shops, textile stores and men peddling cartloads of cucumbers or simit and walk over the Galata Bridge towards the retail melee along Istiklal Caddesi, with its Mavi jean boutiques, bookshops, bars and cafés. A quick diversion to Karaköy Güllüoğlu, which claims to make 'the best baklava in Istanbul', is of course on the agenda. I'd never argue — these guys are from Gaziantep and know a thing or two about baklava. Tanked-up on their syrupy squares of moreishness, I'd wend my way up to Cihangir where the skinny streets are lined with old European-style apartment buildings and antique shops. It's not hard to lose hours rummaging around here so there's no point keeping time.

When my stomach tells me to move on, I'm perfectly poised to drop into Antiocha, a little place run by a friend who hails from the southern town of Antakya near the Syrian border, where the food is legendarily good. The menu is small but well edited and makes a feature of boutique-produced olive oil, cheeses and olives from Antakya, homemade yoghurt and the best beef money can buy. Rarely is shish kebab as juicy and succulent, and the wonderfully flavoured meze (such as *kekik salatasi*, a relish-like assemblage of olives, thyme and olive oil) are veritable flavour explosions.

But then this is Istanbul, so you'll definitely need more than one morning to truly make the most of it.

OCTOPUS WITH POTATOES, OLIVES AND ORANGE-PAPRIKA VINAIGRETTE

INGREDIENTS

1.5 kg (3 lb 5 oz/about 4) octopus, cleaned

4 oregano sprigs

1 fresh bay leaf

2 garlic cloves, bruised

1½ teaspoons whole allspice berries

1 lemon, halved widthways

600 g (1 lb 5 oz) kipfler, or other waxy
   potatoes, peeled

115 g (4 oz/⅔ cup) small black olives

½ cup coriander (cilantro) sprigs, to serve

ORANGE-PAPRIKA VINAIGRETTE

1 orange, peel removed in large strips,
   white pith removed, and cut into
   very fine julienne

500 ml (17 fl oz/2 cups) freshly squeezed
   orange juice

2 tablespoons freshly squeezed lemon juice

1½ teaspoons sweet paprika

2 teaspoons dijon mustard

2 teaspoons sugar

125 ml (4 fl oz/½ cup) extra virgin olive oil

METHOD

To make the orange-paprika vinaigrette, combine the finely sliced orange zest and orange juice in a small saucepan and bring to the boil. Reduce the heat to medium–low and simmer for about 30 minutes, or until the liquid has reduced by about half. Remove from the heat and cool. Whisk the cooled orange reduction with the lemon juice, paprika, mustard and sugar. Add the olive oil in a slow steady stream, whisking constantly. Season with sea salt and freshly ground black pepper, to taste. Set aside until ready to serve.

Place the octopus in a saucepan with the oregano, bay leaf, garlic, allspice and 250 ml (9 fl oz/1 cup) water. Squeeze the lemon to extract the juice, then strain, reserving the skins. Add the juice and skins to the pan. Cover with a tight-fitting lid and cook over medium–low heat for 1½ hours, or until the octopus is very tender and any large suckers easily pull off. Drain the octopus, discarding the lemon skins, herbs and allspice; cool. Pull the large suckers and any thick skin off the octopus, remove the tentacles from the bodies (they will just tear off). Cut the octopus bodies into 1 cm (½ inch) pieces and tentacles into smaller pieces and set aside.

Meanwhile, cook the potatoes in salted boiling water for 7–8 minutes, or until just tender. Drain well, cool to room temperature, then cut widthways into 1 cm (½ inch) thick slices. Combine in a bowl with the octopus and olives; season with sea salt and freshly ground black pepper. Drizzle over the dressing and toss well to combine, then divide among bowls or pile onto a large platter. Scatter over the coriander and serve immediately. **SERVES 6**

BROAD BEAN PUREE WITH EGG SALAD

INGREDIENTS

grilled Turkish bread, to serve

BROAD BEAN PUREE

220 g (7³/₄ oz/1¹/₂ cups) whole dried broad
    (fava) beans

1 brown onion, finely chopped

1 all-purpose potato, such as desiree, peeled
    and chopped

280 g (10 oz/1¹/₂ cups) podded and peeled
    fresh or frozen broad (fava) beans

3 teaspoons sugar

2 tablespoons extra virgin olive oil,
    plus extra, to serve

EGG SALAD

2¹/₂ tablespoons freshly squeezed lemon juice,
    or to taste

1 teaspoon finely grated lemon zest

100 ml (3¹/₂ fl oz) extra virgin olive oil

4 hard-boiled eggs, peeled and coarsely
    chopped

50 g (1³/₄ oz/¹/₃ cup) sundried tomatoes,
    cut into thick strips

2 tablespoons chopped dill

60 g (2¹/₄ oz/2 cups) watercress sprigs

METHOD

To make the broad bean purée, put the dried broad beans in a bowl, cover with cold water and leave to soak overnight. Drain well, then remove and discard the skins. Put the broad beans, onion and potato in a saucepan over medium heat and add just enough water to barely cover; bring slowly to a simmer. Reduce the heat to low and cook for 40 minutes, adding a little extra water if necessary (do not add too much water or the finished purée will not be firm enough). Stir in the fresh or frozen broad beans and continue cooking for 15 minutes, or until the beans are tender. Remove from the heat and cool slightly.

Transfer the bean mixture to a food processor. Add the sugar and olive oil and process to make a smooth purée. Season with sea salt and freshly ground black pepper. Place in a well-oiled 1 litre (35 fl oz/4 cup) capacity terrine mould or loaf (bar) tin, smoothing the surface with the back of a spoon. Cool to room temperature, then cover and refrigerate for 2–3 hours or overnight.

To make the egg salad, combine the lemon juice, lemon zest and olive oil in a bowl and whisk well to combine. Add the egg, sundried tomato, dill and watercress and toss to combine, being careful not to break up the egg too much.

To serve, turn the purée out onto a platter and spoon over the egg salad. Drizzle with olive oil and serve with the grilled Turkish bread passed separately.
SERVES 6

MUHAMARA WITH STUFFED FLAT BREAD

METHOD

To make the muhamara, place the capsicums directly over a low flame and cook for about 10–15 minutes, turning often, until the skin is blackened all over. (Alternatively, cook the capsicums on a barbecue grill heated to high.) Transfer to a bowl, cover with a tea towel (dish towel) and stand until cool enough to handle. Remove the blackened skins and seeds — do not rinse them with water or you will lose flavour. Tear the capsicum flesh into pieces and combine in a food processor with the remaining ingredients to make a coarse paste. Season with sea salt and freshly ground black pepper, then transfer to a bowl, cover with plastic wrap and refrigerate for at least 8 hours for the flavours to develop. Muhamara can be stored in an airtight container in the refrigerator for 4–5 days.

To make the flat bread, combine the sugar and 150 ml (5 fl oz) lukewarm water in a small bowl, then sprinkle over the yeast. Set aside for about 8 minutes, or until foamy, then add another 80 ml (2½ fl oz/⅓ cup) lukewarm water and the olive oil.

Combine the flours and the salt in a bowl, add the yeast mixture, and stir to form a coarse dough. Turn out onto a lightly floured board and knead for 7–8 minutes, or until the dough is smooth and elastic. Cover with plastic wrap and set aside in a warm, draught-free place for 1 hour, or until doubled in size.

Meanwhile combine the feta, olives and oregano in a bowl to make the filling.

Knock back the dough on a lightly floured surface and use a large knife to divide the dough into 12 even-sized pieces. Working with one piece of dough at a time, use a rolling pin to roll each piece into a rough circle with a 14 cm (5½ inch) diameter. Divide the filling between the rounds and use your fingers to bring the edges over the top to enclose the filling and form a ball. Place each ball on a floured surface, seam side down, then gently roll out with a rolling pin to make a circle with a 10–12 cm (4–4½ inch) diameter.

Heat a heavy-based frying pan over low heat and brush the base with a little of the extra olive oil. Cook the flat breads, one or two at a time, for 3–4 minutes on each side, or until a deep golden colour and cooked through.

Serve the muhamara at room temperature with the extra olive oil drizzled over and sprinkled with pistachios, and warm flat bread on the side. **SERVES 6–8**

Note: Pomegranate molasses features in the cooking of southern Turkey where a distinct Middle Eastern influence runs strong. It is made from the boiled-down juice of pomegranates and has a wonderful sweet-tart flavour quite unlike anything else. It is available from most large supermarkets.

MUHAMARA

1 kg (2 lb 4 oz/about 4 large) red capsicums (peppers)

75 g (2¾ oz) day-old rustic bread, cut into small pieces

1 garlic clove, chopped

125 g (4½ oz/1¼ cups) walnut halves, coarsely chopped

1 large pinch dried chilli flakes

1 tablespoon tomato paste (concentrated purée)

2 teaspoons freshly squeezed lemon juice

2 tablespoons pomegranate molasses (see note)

1½ teaspoons caster (superfine) sugar

1 teaspoon ground cumin

2 tablespoons olive oil, plus extra, to serve

chopped pistachios, to serve (optional)

STUFFED FLAT BREAD

1 teaspoon sugar

1½ teaspoons instant dried yeast

1½ tablespoons olive oil, plus extra, for cooking

300 g (10½ oz/2 cups) plain (all-purpose) flour, sifted

150 g (5½ oz/1 cup) wholemeal (whole-wheat) flour, sifted

1 teaspoon salt

150 g (5½ oz/1 cup) crumbled feta cheese

175 g (6 oz/1 cup) pitted green olives, chopped

¼ cup oregano leaves

ALBANIAN LIVER WITH ONION AND PAPRIKA SAUCE

METHOD

To make the onion, vinegar and paprika sauce, heat the olive oil in a large, heavy-based saucepan over medium heat. Add the onion and cook, stirring often, for 12–15 minutes, or until very soft. Add the currants and paprika, stirring well and cook for 1–2 minutes. Add the sugar, vinegar and stock and bring to a simmer, then reduce the heat to low and cook for 20 minutes, or until the onion is very tender and the liquid has reduced. Season with sea salt and freshly ground black pepper.

Cut the liver into 1 cm (½ inch) thick strips. Combine the flour, paprika and chilli powder in a bowl and season well. Add the liver and toss to coat. Heat half of the oil in a large, heavy-based frying pan over medium–high heat. Add half of the liver and cook for 3–4 minutes, turning once, or until golden and cooked through but still a little pink in the middle. Remove to a plate lined with baking paper and keep warm. Repeat with the remaining oil and liver until cooked. Serve immediately with the onion, vinegar and paprika sauce on the side. **SERVES 6**

INGREDIENTS

750 g (1 lb 10 oz) lamb or veal livers, trimmed and fine membrane removed
75 g (2¾ oz/½ cup) plain (all-purpose) flour
2 teaspoons sweet paprika
1 teaspoon chilli powder, or to taste
80 ml (2½ fl oz/⅓ cup) extra virgin olive oil

ONION AND PAPRIKA SAUCE

60 ml (2 fl oz/¼ cup) extra virgin olive oil
800 g (1 lb 12 oz) onions, peeled and thinly sliced
35 g (1¼ oz/¼ cup) currants
2 teaspoons sweet paprika
1 tablespoon caster (superfine) sugar
60 ml (2 fl oz/¼ cup) cider vinegar
310 ml (10¾ fl oz/1¼ cups) chicken stock

WARM PUMPKIN HUMMUS

METHOD

Put the drained chickpeas in a saucepan with enough fresh water to cover. Cook in simmering water for 1 hour, or until very tender. Drain well and cool slightly. Using your hands, rub the chickpeas vigorously to loosen the skins, then remove as many skins as possible (this step may seem fiddly but will greatly improve the texture of the hummus).

Meanwhile, heat the oil in a saucepan over medium heat. Add the pumpkin, cover, and cook for 20–25 minutes, stirring occasionally, until the pumpkin is very tender. Put the hot pumpkin and any cooking juices in a food processor with the chickpeas, garlic, lemon juice and tahini and process until the mixture is well combined and smooth. Season with sea salt, freshly ground black pepper and dried chilli flakes, if using, then serve immediately. **SERVES 6**

INGREDIENTS

275 g (9¾ oz/1¼ cups) dried chickpeas, soaked overnight and drained
60 ml (2 fl oz/¼ cup) extra virgin olive oil
600 g (1 lb 5 oz) butternut pumpkin (squash), peeled, seeded and chopped
2 garlic cloves, crushed
60 ml (2 fl oz/¼ cup) freshly squeezed lemon juice, or to taste
2½ tablespoons tahini
dried chilli flakes, to taste (optional)

BREAKFAST IN VAN

The first time I waddled happily out of the Van Kahvalti Evi (Van Breakfast House) in trendy Cihangir in Istanbul, a restaurant making a feature of the celebrated breakfast foods of Van, I determine to visit that far-flung city near the border with Iran as soon as possible. As I bus in from Doğubeyazit to the north, we start skirting the mighty, azure Lake Van, sparkling with more shades of blue than I knew existed. There's a spectacular show of wild flowers along the foreshore (it's spring), dramatic snow-capped mountains to the south, itinerant bee keepers camped about the roadside and a highway frequently reduced to a crawl by flocks of herding sheep. Upon first appearances the town itself seems bland and utilitarian, but the longer I stay (and the more I return), the more Van grows on me. The atmosphere is friendly and laidback. I always have a great time in Van but it is without doubt the breakfasts that keep me coming back.

Breakfasting is taken so seriously in Van there is even a street, Kahvalti Caddesi (Breakfast Street), devoted to its consumption. Typically, the eateries' windows are littered with tubs of glistening olives, neat chunks of gooey comb honey, elegant folds of *kaymak* (Turkish clotted cream that in these parts is made from sheep's milk), mounds of rich local butter and some interesting variations on a theme of cheese. Included in this is the fabled *otlu peynir*, or 'grassy cheese', so-called on account of the chopped wild mountain herbs that are incorporated into the piquant, white curd. Locals tank up on 'the works', which includes plates of all of the above, plus boiled eggs, wedges of tomato, slices of cucumber and mountains of *ekmek*, a crusty, chewy bread delivered hot from the nearby bakehouse. Hungrier souls order *murtuğa*, eggs scrambled with butter and flour, or *kavut*, a local speciality made by toasting coarse wholemeal flour, then cooking it to a thick porridge with butter, milk and sugar. I've learned to edit my breakfast down to a few, mind-blowing basics and my breakfast of choice involves chewy bread, *kaymak* and honey.

The Turkish word for breakfast, *kahvalti*, means 'before coffee', so tulip-shaped glasses of strong sweet tea are the thing to accompany morning food. Tea and an overloud television blasting out the latest Galatasaray, Beşiktaş or Fernerbahce victory to all who care. In this soccer-crazed nation, all (except me) care deeply. Even at breakfast time.

Strictly speaking, this is more of a breakfast dish than a meze but you could easily serve it as a meze by omitting the eggs. If you can't find sujuk, a wonderfully spicy, dry Turkish sausage, you can substitute a not-too-hot mergeuz or chorizo instead.

SPICY LENTILS BAKED WITH EGGS AND SUJUK

METHOD

Put the lentils in a saucepan and add enough cold water to just cover. Bring to a simmer and cook for 10 minutes, or until partially cooked. Drain well and set aside.

Heat half the olive oil in a saucepan over medium heat. Add the onion, carrot, celery, garlic, bay leaves and cinnamon, and cook for 6–7 minutes, or until the onion has softened. Add the paprika, chilli and tomato paste and cook, stirring, for 1–2 minutes, or until fragrant. Add the tomato, stock and par-cooked lentils and stir well to combine. Bring to a simmer, cover, then reduce the heat to low and cook for 20 minutes, or until the lentils are tender. Season with sea salt and freshly ground black pepper, to taste. Discard the cinnamon stick and bay leaves.

Preheat the oven to 180°C (350°F/Gas 4). Divide the lentil mixture between four 625 ml (21½ fl oz/2½ cup) capacity ovenproof baking dishes. Break two eggs into each dish over the lentil mixture and bake for 15–20 minutes, or until the eggs are set.

Meanwhile, heat the remaining oil in a large frying pan over medium heat. Add slices of sujuk to the pan and cook for 3–4 minutes on each side, or until golden. Divide among the dishes and serve immediately. **SERVES 4**

Note: Red Persian lentils are small and nutty in flavour, and much like puy lentils they hold their shape perfectly when cooked. They are available from speciality grocery stores. You can use ordinary brown lentils if red Persian lentils are unavailable.

INGREDIENTS

225 g (8 oz/1¼ cups) red Persian lentils (see note) or brown lentils

80 ml (2½ fl oz/⅓ cup) olive oil

1 large onion, finely chopped

1 carrot, peeled and finely chopped

1 celery stick, finely chopped

3 garlic cloves, finely chopped

2 fresh bay leaves

1 cinnamon stick

2 teaspoons sweet paprika

1 teaspoon dried chilli flakes, or to taste

2 tablespoons tomato paste (concentrated purée)

800 g (1 lb 12 oz/3¼ cups) tin chopped tomatoes

500 ml (17 fl oz/2 cups) chicken stock

8 eggs

600 g (1 lb 5 oz) sujuk (Turkish sausage), cut into 1 cm (½ inch) thick slices

CABBAGE, PRAWN AND RICE DOLMAS

INGREDIENTS

1 green cabbage

100 g (3½ oz/½ cup) long-grain white rice

800 g (1 lb 12 oz) raw king prawns (shrimp), peeled, deveined and chopped

500 g (1 lb 2 oz) prawn (shrimp) meat, finely chopped

1 onion, very finely chopped

2 garlic cloves, finely chopped

2 tablespoons tomato paste (concentrated purée)

60 g (2¼ oz/⅓ cup) small capers, drained

1 teaspoon paprika

2½ tablespoons chopped flat-leaf (Italian) parsley

2½ tablespoons chopped dill

500 ml (17 fl oz/2 cups) chicken stock

extra virgin olive oil, to serve

chopped dill and lemon wedges, to serve

METHOD

Discard the tough outer cabbage leaves. Carefully remove the large outer cabbage leaves, cutting in half along the central vein — you need about 12 leaves in total. Bring a large saucepan of salted water to the boil and blanch the leaves, in batches, for 3 minutes each, or until softened. Drain well and set aside to cool; pat dry with paper towels to remove any excess liquid.

Soak the rice in a bowl of cold water for 10 minutes, then drain well. Combine in a bowl with the prawn meat, onion, garlic, tomato paste, capers, paprika, parsley and dill. Season with sea salt and freshly ground black pepper, then use your hands to mix everything together.

Cut each half cabbage leaf in half. Working with one piece at a time, place on a work surface with a long edge facing towards you. Place a heaped tablespoon of the rice mixture along the edge, leaving a slight border, then fold the shorter edges over and roll up into a finger, about 4 cm (1½ inches) long — don't roll the dolmas too tightly as they need a little room to expand. You may not need all of the cabbage leaves.

Use the remaining leaves to line a saucepan large enough to fit the dolmas in a single layer. Arrange the dolmas carefully in the pan, seam side down. Pour over the stock. Place a plate over the dolmas to keep them slightly weighted down, then cover the pan with a lid. Place over medium heat, bring to a simmer, then reduce the heat to low and cook for 1 hour. Remove the pan from the heat and cool the dolmas slightly then, when cool enough to handle, carefully remove them from the pan and cool to room temperature. Serve with the olive oil drizzled over the top and scattered with the dill and the lemon wedges on the side.

MAKES ABOUT 30

I can't say I ate green tomatoes and celery prepared this way in Turkey, but the zingy flavours are a perfect foil for fried cheese, which I did enjoy on the Aegean coast. In these parts, the food is influenced by neighbouring Greece — although any Turk will tell you that *they* taught the Greeks to cook.

FRIED HALOUMI WITH GREEN TOMATO AND CELERY RELISH

METHOD

To make the green tomato and celery relish, heat the olive oil in a saucepan over medium heat. Add the onion and garlic and cook for 5 minutes, or until softened. Add the tomato, celery, capers and cinnamon, cover, and cook for 5 minutes, stirring occasionally until the tomatoes have softened slightly and released some juices. Add the honey, vinegar and allspice, bring back to a simmer and cook, uncovered, for 10 minutes. Remove from the heat, cool to room temperature, then season with sea salt and freshly ground black pepper. Remove the cinnamon stick and set the relish aside until ready to serve.

Just before you are ready to serve, cook the haloumi. Heat the oil in a large frying pan over medium heat. Dust the haloumi lightly in the seasoned flour, shaking off any excess. Add to the pan in a single layer and cook, in batches if necessary, for 3 minutes on each side or until golden. Divide among warmed plates or arrange on a platter with the lemon wedges. Serve the green tomato and celery relish on the side scattered with the dill. **SERVES 6**

INGREDIENTS

600 g (1 lb 5 oz) haloumi, sliced into
    12 x 1 cm ($\frac{1}{2}$ inch) thick pieces
seasoned flour, for dusting
60 ml (2 fl oz/$\frac{1}{4}$ cup) olive oil
lemon wedges, to serve

GREEN TOMATO AND CELERY RELISH

2$\frac{1}{2}$ tablespoons extra virgin olive oil
2 onions, very finely chopped
3 garlic cloves, finely sliced
600 g (1 lb 5 oz) green tomatoes, cut into
    1 cm ($\frac{1}{2}$ inch) pieces
2 celery sticks, cut on the diagonal into
    5 mm ($\frac{1}{4}$ inch) thick slices
35 g (1$\frac{1}{4}$ oz/$\frac{1}{4}$ cup) capers, drained
1 cinnamon stick
1$\frac{1}{2}$ tablespoons honey
2 tablespoons white wine vinegar
1 teaspoon ground allspice
2$\frac{1}{2}$ tablespoons chopped dill

FISH MARINATED IN VINEGAR, TOMATO, OREGANO AND ALLSPICE

INGREDIENTS

1.25 kg (2 lb 12 oz/about 12) whole skinless, boneless garfish, cleaned and patted dry

plain (all-purpose) flour, for dusting

olive oil, for frying

250 ml (9 fl oz/1 cup) red wine vinegar

250 g (9 oz/1 cup) tomato passata (puréed tomatoes)

500 ml (17 fl oz/2 cups) extra virgin olive oil

60 ml (2 fl oz/¼ cup) honey

4 dried oregano sprigs

6 garlic cloves, bruised

1 teaspoon ground allspice

METHOD

Dust the fish lightly in the flour, shaking off any excess. Heat a little olive oil in a large, heavy-based frying pan over medium heat. Cook the fish, in batches, for 2–3 minutes on each side, or until just cooked through. Remove to a tray while cooking the remaining fish, adding more oil to the pan as needed.

Combine the vinegar, tomato passata, extra virgin olive oil, honey, oregano, garlic and allspice in a saucepan and slowly bring to a simmer. Reduce the heat to low and cook for 2–3 minutes, then remove from the heat and cool slightly.

Arrange the fish in a large ceramic dish, season well with sea salt and freshly ground black pepper, and pour over the vinegar mixture. Cool to room temperature, cover with plastic wrap and refrigerate overnight. Bring to room temperature to serve. **SERVES 6–8**

TUNA IN OLIVE OIL

INGREDIENTS

800 g (1 lb 12 oz) tuna steaks, blood line trimmed

2 teaspoons coriander seeds

1½ teaspoons cumin seeds

1 tablespoon caster (superfine) sugar

1 tablespoon sea salt

1 lemon

1 teaspoon freshly ground black pepper

375 ml (13 fl oz/1½ cups) extra virgin olive oil

METHOD

Using a sharp knife, cut the tuna steaks on a slight diagonal into pieces about 4 cm (1½ inches) wide. Toast the coriander and cumin seeds in a dry small, heavy-based frying pan over medium–low heat for 2–3 minutes, shaking the pan occasionally, or until fragrant. Coarsely grind the spices using a mortar and pestle or an electric spice grinder.

Generously oil the base and sides of a 26 x 15 cm (10½ x 6 inch) ceramic or glass dish. Arrange the fish in a single layer so they slightly overlap and sprinkle over the spices, sugar and salt. Cover with plastic wrap and stand at room temperature for 30 minutes.

Meanwhile, preheat the oven to 120°C (235°F/Gas ½). Finely grate the lemon and sprinkle the zest over the tuna. Squeeze and strain the lemon juice then pour over the tuna. Add the pepper and drizzle over the olive oil — it should just cover the fish. Cover the dish tightly with foil and bake for about 30 minutes, or until the tuna is just cooked through. Remove from the oven and allow to cool in the oil; serve at room temperature. The tuna will keep, stored in the oil, covered and refrigerated, for up to 5 days. **SERVES 6–8**

SOUPS

It's fair to say Turks love soups. They can literally start and end the day with a soup. Lentil soup (*mercimek çorbası*) is a beloved, and fortifying, breakfast staple, which often gets wolfed down on the run accompanied by handfuls of crusty bread. Tripe soup (*işkembe çorbası*) is a late-night favourite used to revive tired bodies from an evening of heavy partying. Turkish soups are generally light and simple affairs that make a feature of just one or two main ingredients — think rice and tomato, a selection of fish, or yoghurt and barley.

Yoghurt is a Turkish staple — indeed, it is a Turkish word. It is used in soups, as it is here, and served alongside kebabs, köfte and other meat dishes, also forming the basis of many dips and spreads. A liaison of egg yolk and lemon juice is a typical addition to a Turkish soup, thickening the liquid and adding a silky richness.

YOGHURT, MINT AND BARLEY SOUP

METHOD

Put the barley, bay leaf and stock in a saucepan over medium–low heat and bring to a simmer. Partially cover the pan and cook for 30 minutes, or until the barley is tender.

Combine the yoghurt, dried mint, egg yolks and lemon zest in a bowl and whisk well to combine. In a separate smaller bowl, mix together the cornflour and lemon juice to form a smooth paste. Stir the cornflour mixture into the yoghurt mixture. Use a ladle to transfer about 500 ml (17 fl oz/2 cups) of the hot stock mixture into the yoghurt mixture and stir to combine well. Pour this back into the stock in the pan then, stirring constantly, continue to cook the soup over medium heat until it just comes back to a simmer and thickens. Serve immediately sprinkled with some lemon zest. **SERVES 4–6**

INGREDIENTS

110 g (3¾ oz/½ cup) pearl barley

1 fresh bay leaf

1 litre (35 fl oz/4 cups) chicken stock

500 g (1 lb 2 oz/2 cups) Greek-style yoghurt

2 teaspoons dried mint

3 egg yolks

2 teaspoons finely grated lemon zest, plus
  extra, to serve

1 tablespoon cornflour (cornstarch)

2½ tablespoons freshly squeezed lemon juice

LENTIL, SILVERBEET AND LAMB KÖFTE SOUP

INGREDIENTS

220 g (7³/₄ oz/1 cup) dried chickpeas, soaked
    overnight and drained

60 ml (2 fl oz/¹/₄ cup) olive oil

2 onions, finely chopped

3 garlic cloves, crushed

2 tablespoons tomato paste
    (concentrated purée)

2 tablespoons Turkish pepper paste
    (see note page 13)

2¹/₂ teaspoons dried oregano

1 fresh bay leaf

250 g (9 oz/1¹/₃ cups) brown lentils

2.25 litres (80 fl oz) chicken stock

1 bunch silverbeet (Swiss chard), trimmed,
    stems and ribs removed and leaves
    finely chopped

lemon wedges, to serve

Greek-style yoghurt, to serve

dried chilli flakes, to serve

extra virgin olive oil, to serve

KÖFTE

90 g (3¹/₄ oz/¹/₂ cup) fine burghul (bulgur)

75 g (2³/₄ oz/¹/₂ cup) plain (all-purpose) flour

200 g (7 oz) minced (ground) lamb

2¹/₂ teaspoons tomato paste
    (concentrated purée)

¹/₂ teaspoon ground allspice

¹/₂ teaspoon ground cinnamon

METHOD

Put the chickpeas in a saucepan with just enough water to cover. Bring to the boil, then reduce the heat to low and simmer for 1 hour, or until tender. Drain the chickpeas, cover and reserve.

Meanwhile, to make the köfte, rinse the burghul and drain well, using your hands to squeeze out as much excess liquid as possible. Combine in a food processor with the flour, lamb, tomato paste, allspice and cinnamon; season with sea salt and freshly ground black pepper. Process until the mixture is smooth and elastic. Take scant teaspoonfuls of the mixture at a time and roll into neat balls using your hands. Place on a baking tray lined with baking paper and refrigerate until needed.

Heat the olive oil in a large saucepan over medium heat. Add the onion and garlic and cook for 5–6 minutes, or until softened. Add the tomato paste, pepper paste, oregano and bay leaf and cook, stirring, for another 1 minute. Add the lentils and chicken stock, bring to the boil, then reduce the heat to low and simmer for 50 minutes, or until the lentils are tender. Add the chickpeas and cook for 3–4 minutes to heat through, then stir in the silverbeet. Bring the soup back to a gentle simmer and carefully stir in the köfte; cook over low heat for 6–7 minutes, or until the silverbeet has wilted and the köfte are cooked through. Season with sea salt and freshly ground black pepper and serve the soup in large bowls with the lemon wedges, yoghurt, chilli flakes and olive oil passed separately. **SERVES 6**

TOMATO, CAPSICUM AND RICE SOUP WITH GOAT'S CURD AND CORIANDER

INGREDIENTS

1 kg (2 lb 4 oz) very ripe tomatoes, chopped

2½ tablespoons extra virgin olive oil,
    plus extra, to serve

1 onion, finely chopped

2 garlic cloves, crushed

2 large red capsicums (peppers), seeded,
    membrane removed and finely chopped

1½ tablespoons Turkish pepper paste
    (see note page 13)

½ teaspoon dried chilli flakes, or to taste

2 teaspoons sweet paprika

80 g (2¾ oz/⅓ cup) medium-grain rice

1 tablespoon sugar

625 ml (21½ fl oz/2½ cups) chicken stock

125 g (4½ oz) goat's curd

chopped coriander (cilantro) leaves, to serve

METHOD

Put the tomato into a food processor and process until a smooth purée forms.

Heat the olive oil in a large saucepan over medium heat. Add the onion and garlic and cook for 5–6 minutes, or until softened. Add the capsicum and cook for 10 minutes, stirring often, until softened. Add the pepper paste, chilli flakes and paprika and cook, stirring, for 1 minute, then add the rice, sugar, chicken stock and tomato purée and stir well to combine. Bring to a simmer, then cook over medium–low heat for 20 minutes, or until the rice is very tender. Season with sea salt and freshly ground black pepper. Divide among serving bowls. Divide the goat's curd among the bowls, sprinkle with the coriander, drizzle with a little extra olive oil and serve immediately. **SERVES 4-6**

Turkey is the third largest producer of pistachios in the world. The fattest, greenest, sweetest nuts are grown around the southern Turkish city of Gaziantep. Large piles and sacks of nuts are on display at the local markets, available in all sizes and grades, with vendors offering small handfuls to taste as you pass by.

CHICKEN AND PISTACHIO SOUP

METHOD

Put the whole chicken, carrot, celery, bay leaf and half of the onion in a saucepan. Add just enough cold water to cover and bring to a gentle simmer. Cook over low heat for 45 minutes, or until the chicken is tender; do not allow the liquid to simmer hard or the chicken will be tough. Remove the chicken and cool. Strain and reserve the cooking liquid, discarding the vegetables — you should have 1.5 litres (52 fl oz/6 cups) stock; add extra water if necessary. Remove the chicken meat, discarding the skin, fat and bones. Finely shred the chicken and set aside.

Melt the butter in a saucepan over medium–low heat, then add the remaining onion and cook for 8 minutes, or until softened. Add the flour and cook for 3 minutes, stirring to combine. Add 250 ml (9 fl oz/1 cup) of the reserved cooking liquid and stir constantly until the mixture has boiled and thickened. Continue adding the stock, 1 cup at a time, and stirring constantly between additions, until all the stock is used and the soup is quite thick.

Place the pistachios into a food processor and process until very finely ground. Add the milk, cream, chicken meat and pistachios to the soup and heat gently until just simmering; do not allow the soup to boil or it will curdle; season with sea salt and freshly ground black pepper.

Divide the soup among bowls and sprinkle with the extra chopped pistachios, to serve. **SERVES 4–6**

INGREDIENTS

1 kg (2 lb 4 oz) whole chicken

1 carrot, chopped

1 celery stick, chopped

1 bay leaf

2 onions, chopped

60 g (2¼ oz) butter

50 g (1¾ oz/⅓ cup) plain (all-purpose) flour

100 g (3½ oz/¾ cup) unsalted pistachios, plus extra, chopped, to serve

125 ml (4 fl oz/½ cup) full-cream (whole) milk

125 ml (4 fl oz/½ cup) pouring (whipping) cream

CELERIAC, SAFFRON AND MUSSEL SOUP

METHOD

Sprinkle the saffron threads into a small bowl with 80 ml ($2\frac{1}{2}$ fl oz/$\frac{1}{3}$ cup) hot water and set aside for 1 hour, or until the liquid is a deep yellow colour.

Put the stock in a large saucepan and bring to the boil. Add half of the mussels, cover the pan, and cook over high heat for about 3 minutes, or until the mussels have opened. Remove to a bowl using a slotted spoon and repeat with the remaining mussels until all are cooked. Discard any mussels that do not open. Reserve the cooking liquid. Remove the meat, discarding the shells and reserve any juices in a bowl.

Meanwhile, heat the olive oil in a large saucepan over medium heat. Add the onion, garlic and celery and cook for 5–6 minutes, stirring often, until softened. Add the celeriac, potato and bay leaf, stirring to combine well, then cover and cook for 10–12 minutes, or until the vegetables have softened. Add the reserved stock, any mussel juices and the saffron mixture, and bring the soup to a simmer. Cook, uncovered, over medium–low heat for 8–10 minutes. Add the mussel meat to the pan, season with sea salt and freshly ground black pepper, and continue cooking for about 2 minutes, or until the mussels are just heated through. Stir in the parsley and serve immediately. **SERVES 4-6**

INGREDIENTS

$\frac{1}{2}$ teaspoon saffron threads

1 litre (35 fl oz/4 cups) fish or chicken stock

2 kg (4 lb 8 oz) black mussels, beards removed and shells scrubbed

$2\frac{1}{2}$ tablespoons extra virgin olive oil

2 onions, chopped

3 garlic cloves, finely chopped

3 celery sticks, cut into 5 mm ($\frac{1}{4}$ inch) pieces

700 g (1 lb 9 oz) celeriac, trimmed, peeled and cut into 5 mm ($\frac{1}{4}$ inch) thick slices

400 g (14 oz) all-purpose potatoes, cut into 1 cm ($\frac{1}{2}$ inch) pieces

1 fresh bay leaf

$\frac{1}{2}$ cup flat-leaf (Italian) parsley leaves, coarsely chopped

TANDOOR BREAD AND WILD HERBS IN A KURDISH VILLAGE

I hire an English-speaking driver to take me somewhere — anywhere — where I can observe everyday village life. His choice is a village near the small town of Gevaş, about sixty kilometres south of Van. It turns out to be tiny, Kurdish, and has a dreamy setting among huge old trees at the base of steep hills. A small stream bubbles past the squat sand-coloured stone houses and the whole place is a hub of activity. Food activity!

First I'm taken into a dark, smoke-filled room where women are hard at work around a tandoor oven — a cylindrical clay oven set into a hole in the ground (in Turkish its name is *gömme tandir*, meaning buried tandoor) and fired by wood. Unlike more Westernised parts of Turkey, here the tandoor is a necessity — most of the old homes don't have their own ovens and households share in the preparation of items such as bread. I watch as one woman scoops up handfuls of sloppy dough from a large tub and shapes them into perfect, round balls. Another deftly rolls the dough into thin discs. These are then moistened slightly and slapped against the side of the tandoor with the aid of a round, padded block. They stick perfectly and are retrieved five minutes later, crisp, golden and steaming. It's repetitive, back-breaking work as they make dozens of loaves at a time, enough to feed several families for a week.

Outside, a young girl is washing chive-like herbs that emit a strong, garlic-like fragrance. This is the herb *sarmisakotu*, used to flavour the famous *otlu peynir* or 'grassy cheese' for which Van is famous. The manufacture of *otlu peynir* is a highly seasonal endeavour. The herbs are picked in spring from the hills surrounding Van, where they grow wild, and the milk (mainly from sheep) is most plentiful then too. Throughout June the villagers make cheese for their own consumption — it is brined then aged in tubs in the ground for about six months, where it becomes progressively more pungent, crumbly and salty. In July and August they make more cheese but this is to sell.

Before we leave we dine on *ayran asi*, the yoghurt-based soup that's enjoyed throughout the Kurdish south-east. It's served warm and is thick with chickpeas, soft boiled wheat, spinach and herbs. It's tasty, nourishing food served with chunks of the tandoor bread we watched being made earlier. We're sent home with a floppy round of bread each, wrapped in newspaper and still faintly warm and smoky from the oven.

RED LENTIL SOUP WITH MINTED EGGPLANT

METHOD

Heat 2 tablespoons of the olive oil in a large saucepan over medium heat. Add the onion and cook for 6–7 minutes, or until softened. Add the lentils and stock, then bring to a simmer, skimming the surface to remove any impurities. Reduce the heat to low, partially cover the pan, and simmer for 40–50 minutes, or until the lentils are very soft and have collapsed. Add the lemon juice and season with sea salt and freshly ground black pepper.

Meanwhile, sprinkle the salt over the chopped eggplant in a colander and set aside for 20 minutes. Rinse the eggplant well, then drain and pat dry on paper towels. Heat the remaining olive oil in a large, heavy-based frying pan over medium–high heat. Add the eggplant and cook for 5–6 minutes, turning often, until golden and tender. Add the garlic and cook for 2 minutes, then add the mint and paprika and cook for another 2 minutes, or until fragrant.

To serve, divide the soup among bowls and spoon over the eggplant and garlic mixture and scatter with the mint. **SERVES 6**

INGREDIENTS

150 ml (5 fl oz) extra virgin olive oil

2 onions, finely chopped

625 g (1 lb 6 oz/2½ cups) red lentils

2.5 litres (88 fl oz) chicken or vegetable stock

60 ml (2 fl oz/¼ cup) freshly squeezed lemon juice, or to taste

2 tablespoons salt

500 g (1 lb 2 oz/about 1 large) eggplant (aubergine), cut into 1 cm (½ inch) pieces

2 garlic cloves, crushed

3 teaspoons dried mint

2½ teaspoons sweet paprika

3 tablespoons chopped fresh mint, to serve

BREAD, PASTRY AND PASTA

Bread plays such a significant role in Turkey that it is traditionally regarded as sacred and wasting the leftovers, a sin. No Turkish meal is complete without bread, typically baked to golden crustiness in wood-fired ovens. Both leavened and unleavened breads feature in Turkish baking, as do myriad pastries, particularly börek, the making of which is considered something of an art form. Yufka dough, a traditional dough, somewhat thicker than filo pastry, forms the basis of many Turkish pastries and takes skill and patience to perfect — ideally it is rolled out using a long, thin rolling pin called an *olava*.

LAHMACUN

1 red onion, finely chopped

2 garlic cloves, finely chopped

600 g (1 lb 5 oz) minced (ground) lamb

1½ tablespoons Turkish pepper paste
   (see note page 13)

2 ripe tomatoes, quartered, seeded
   and chopped

1 red capsicum (pepper), seeded, membrane
   removed and finely chopped

1 handful flat-leaf (Italian) parsley,
   leaves chopped

1 handful coriander (cilantro) leaves, chopped

½ teaspoon dried chilli flakes, plus extra,
   to serve

lemon wedges, to serve

DOUGH

1 pinch sugar

2 teaspoons dried yeast

600 g (1 lb 5 oz/4 cups) plain (all-purpose)
   flour, plus extra, for dusting

2 teaspoons salt

METHOD

To make the dough, combine the sugar and 125 ml (4 fl oz/½ cup) lukewarm water in a small bowl, then sprinkle over the yeast. Set aside for about 8 minutes, or until foamy, then add another 375 ml (13 fl oz/1½ cups) lukewarm water.

Combine the flour and salt in a bowl, then add the yeast mixture and stir to form a coarse dough. Turn out onto a lightly floured surface and knead for 5 minutes, or until the dough is smooth and elastic. Roll the dough into a ball and place in a lightly oiled bowl, turning to coat. Cover with plastic wrap and set aside in a warm, draught-free place for 1 hour, or until doubled in size.

Meanwhile, combine the onion, garlic, lamb and pepper paste in a bowl and season with sea salt and freshly ground black pepper. Using your hands, knead together for 5 minutes, or until very well combined — the mixture should be smooth and sticky. Add the tomato, capsicum, parsley, coriander and chilli, and gently knead until well combined.

Preheat the oven to 220°C (425°F/Gas 7). Line two baking trays with baking paper. Knock back the dough on a lightly floured work surface and divide it into 12 even-sized balls. Roll each ball into a 25 x 14 cm (10 x 5½ inch) oval using a rolling pin. Spread each oval thinly with some of the lamb mixture, leaving a 1 cm (½ inch) border around the edge.

Gently transfer the lahmacun to the prepared trays and bake, in batches, for 10–15 minutes, or until the dough is golden and crisp. Serve hot with the lemon wedges and extra chilli flakes on the side. **MAKES 12**

SWEET TAHINI SPIRALS

METHOD

To make the dough, combine the sugar and 125 ml (4 fl oz/$\frac{1}{2}$ cup) lukewarm water in a small bowl, then sprinkle over the yeast. Set aside for about 8 minutes, or until foamy. Combine the lukewarm milk and the beaten eggs, then add to the yeast mixture with another 2 tablespoons lukewarm water and the olive oil, stirring well to combine.

Combine the flour and salt in a bowl, then add the yeast mixture and stir to form a coarse dough. Turn out onto a lightly floured surface and knead for 5 minutes, or until the dough is smooth and elastic. Roll the dough into a ball and place in a lightly oiled bowl, turning to coat. Cover with plastic wrap and set aside in a warm, draught-free place for 1 hour, or until doubled in size.

Meanwhile, put the tahini, caster sugar and the extra egg in a bowl, mixing until well combined — the mixture will become quite thick.

Knock back the dough on a lightly floured work surface and divide it into 12 even-sized balls. Working with one ball at a time, roll each out into a circle with an 18 cm (7 inch) diameter using a rolling pin. Spread a tablespoon of the tahini mixture on each round, leaving a 1 cm ($\frac{1}{2}$ inch) border around the edge. Roll up each to form a long sausage shape and continue to roll until it's about 30 cm (12 inches) long. Use your hands to shape each sausage into a tight spiral — each spiral should be about 10 cm (4 inches) in diameter — then flatten slightly. Transfer to lightly greased baking trays, cover loosely with a tea towel (dish towel), and set aside for about 30 minutes, or until puffy.

Preheat the oven to 220°C (425°F/Gas 7). Brush the tops of each spiral with the egg yolk mixture and sprinkle lightly with sesame seeds. Bake for 30 minutes, or until golden and cooked through. Transfer to a wire rack to cool. Tahini spirals are best eaten on the day of making but will keep, frozen in an airtight container, for up to 1 month. **MAKES 12**

INGREDIENTS

1 large pinch sugar

3 teaspoons dried yeast

170 ml (5$\frac{1}{2}$ fl oz/$\frac{2}{3}$ cup) lukewarm milk

2 eggs, lightly beaten, plus 1 extra

2$\frac{1}{2}$ tablespoons extra virgin olive oil

600 g (1 lb 5 oz/4 cups) plain (all-purpose) flour

2 teaspoons salt

270 g (9$\frac{1}{2}$ oz/1 cup) tahini

220 g (7$\frac{3}{4}$ oz/1 cup) caster (superfine) sugar

1 egg yolk whisked with 1$\frac{1}{2}$ tablespoons water

sesame seeds, for sprinkling

LAMB, LENTIL AND MINT FILO PIES

INGREDIENTS

140 g (5 oz/³/₄ cup) brown lentils

2 tablespoons olive oil

1 large onion, finely chopped

2 garlic cloves, finely chopped

400 g (14 oz) minced (ground) lamb

2 tablespoons Turkish pepper paste
 (see note page 13)

2 teaspoons sweet paprika

¹/₄ cup chopped mint

¹/₄ cup chopped flat-leaf (Italian) parsley

60 g (2¹/₄ oz/¹/₂ cup) crumbled goat's cheese
 (optional)

18 sheets filo pastry

125 g (4¹/₂ oz) butter, melted

Greek-style yoghurt, to serve

METHOD

Put the lentils in a saucepan and add enough cold water to just cover. Bring to a simmer over medium–low heat and cook for 35–40 minutes, or until tender. Drain well.

Meanwhile, heat the olive oil in a large, heavy-based frying pan over medium heat. Add the onion and garlic and cook for 5–6 minutes, or until softened. Add the lamb and cook for 12–15 minutes, stirring often to break up the meat, until the lamb is browned and all excess liquid has evaporated — the meat needs to be quite dry. Add the pepper paste and paprika and cook for 2 minutes, stirring well. Remove from the heat and stir in the mint, parsley and goat's cheese, if using. Cool to room temperature.

Preheat the oven to 180°C (350°F/Gas 4) and line a baking tray with baking paper. Lay the filo sheets on a clean work surface and cover with a damp tea towel (dish towel) to prevent them from drying out while you work. Take one sheet of filo pastry and sit it with the long edge closest to you. Brush all over with melted butter then place another sheet of pastry on top. Brush with melted butter then place another sheet of pastry over it. Brush the top layer with butter and spoon a thin line of the lamb mixture in a strip down the long side of pastry nearest you, leaving a 2 cm (³/₄ inch) border at each short end. Roll up lengthways to form a skinny log, then shape the log into a tight spiral.

Transfer each spiral to the prepared trays and repeat with the remaining pastry and filling to make six spirals in total. Brush the remaining melted butter over the top of each spiral and bake in the oven for 35 minutes, or until deep golden. Serve hot with yoghurt on the side. **MAKES 6**

The Turks have many flat breads in their repertoire, both leavened and unleavened. This one is inspired by *sac ekmeği* (a sac is large convex griddle that originated in early nomadic life when cooking apparatus needed to be portable). A large heavy-based, cast-iron frying pan works well in the absence of a sac.

FLAT BREAD

METHOD

Combine the sugar and 100 ml (3½ fl oz) lukewarm water in a small bowl and sprinkle over the yeast. Set aside for about 8 minutes, or until foamy, then add 300 ml (10½ fl oz) lukewarm water.

Combine the flour and salt in a bowl, then add the yeast mixture and stir to form a coarse dough. Turn out onto a lightly floured surface and knead for 5 minutes, or until the dough is smooth and elastic. Roll the dough into a ball and place in a lightly oiled bowl, turning to coat. Cover with plastic wrap and set aside in a warm, draught-free place for 1 hour, or until doubled in size.

Knock back the dough on a lightly floured work surface and divide it into 12 even-sized balls. Roll each ball into a circle with a 24 cm (9½ inch) diameter, using a rolling pin. Heat a large non-stick frying pan over medium heat and cook the flat breads, one at a time, for 3 minutes on each side, or until cooked through and just coloured. Remove to a plate to keep warm while you cook the remaining flat breads. Serve warm or at room temperature. Flat breads are best served on the day of making but will keep, frozen in an airtight plastic bag, for up to 4 weeks. **MAKES 12**

INGREDIENTS

1 teaspoon caster (superfine) sugar

1½ teaspoons dried yeast

600 g (1 lb 5 oz/4 cups) plain
    (all-purpose) flour

1½ teaspoons salt

SILVERBEET, FETA AND SULTANA PIDE

Prepare the pide dough following the instructions on page 85 and set aside to rest for 1 hour, or until doubled in size, as the recipe directs.

Finely chop the silverbeet stems and coarsely chop the leaves. Heat the olive oil in a large saucepan over medium heat. Add the onion and garlic and cook for 5 minutes, or until softened. Add the sultanas and silverbeet stems, cover the pan, and cook for 10 minutes, stirring occasionally, until the stems are soft. Coarsely chop the spinach stems and leaves, then add to the pan with the silverbeet leaves, cover, and cook for 3 minutes, or until the spinach has wilted. Season with sea salt and freshly ground black pepper, then remove from the heat and cool slightly. Stir in the feta.

Preheat the oven to 200°C (400°F/Gas 6) and lightly grease two large baking trays. Knock back the dough on a lightly floured work surface and divide the dough into eight even-sized pieces. Working with one piece of dough at a time, roll each piece into a 25 x 16 cm (10 x 6¼ inch) oval, using a rolling pin. Place one-sixth of the filling in the middle of each oval, leaving a 2.5 cm (1 inch) border around the edge, then pull the dough up around the edges to partially cover the filling, pleating the edge. Transfer to the prepared trays, brush the top and side with the egg yolk mixture and bake, in batches, for 15–20 minutes, or until the dough is deep golden and the filling is bubbling. Serve hot or warm. **MAKES 8**

Variation: To make the beef and kashkaval filling, cut the steak into 1 cm (½ inch) pieces and set aside. Heat half of the olive oil in a large frying pan over medium–high heat. Add the meat and cook for 5 minutes, stirring often, until browned. Remove from the heat and set aside.

Heat the remaining oil in a saucepan over medium heat. Add the onion and garlic and cook for 5–6 minutes, stirring often, until softened. Add the pepper paste, tomato paste, paprika, oregano and chilli flakes, if using, and cook for 1–2 minutes, or until fragrant. Add the meat, tomato and 60 ml (2 fl oz/¼ cup) water. Bring to a simmer and cook over low heat for 50 minutes, or until the meat is very tender and the liquid has reduced. Season with sea salt and freshly ground black pepper then remove from the heat and cool to room temperature.

Roll and shape the pide as the recipe directs above, but use the cheese as the filling and spoon the meat over the top once you have pleated the dough. Brush with the egg yolk mixture and bake, in batches, for 15–20 minutes, or until the dough is deep golden. **MAKES 8**

1 portion pide dough (see page 85)

SILVERBEET, FETA AND SULTANA FILLING

600 g (1 lb 5 oz) silverbeet (Swiss chard), 6 cm (2½ inches) stems trimmed

2½ tablespoons extra virgin olive oil

1 large onion, finely chopped

3 garlic cloves, finely chopped

60 g (2¼ oz/½ cup) sultanas (golden raisins)

600 g (1 lb 5 oz) spinach, 3 cm (1¼ inch) trimmed from stems

200 g (7 oz/1⅓ cups) crumbled feta cheese

1 egg yolk beaten with 1½ tablespoons water

BEEF AND KASHKAVAL FILLING (VARIATION)

1 kg (2 lb 4 oz) beef oyster blade or chuck steak

80 ml (2½ fl oz/⅓ cup) olive oil

1 large onion, chopped

2 garlic cloves, crushed

1½ tablespoons Turkish pepper paste (see note page 13)

1 tablespoon tomato paste (concentrated purée)

2 teaspoons paprika

2½ tablespoons oregano leaves

1 teaspoon dried chilli flakes (optional)

400 g (14 oz/1⅔ cup) tin chopped tomatoes

300 g (10½ oz/2 cups) grated kashkaval cheese (see note page 74)

1 egg yolk beaten with 1½ tablespoons water

CHEESE AND POTATO FILO ROLLS

INGREDIENTS

650 g (1 lb 7 oz) all-purpose potatoes, such
    as jersey cream, peeled and quartered
2 tablespoons extra virgin olive oil
1 onion, finely chopped
1 garlic clove, crushed
200 g (7 oz/1⅓ cups) crumbled feta cheese
½ teaspoon ground allspice
2½ tablespoons chopped mint
2½ tablespoons chopped flat-leaf
    (Italian) parsley
1 egg, lightly beaten
14 sheets filo pastry
175 g (6 oz) butter, melted
nigella seeds, for sprinkling

METHOD

Cook the potato in salted boiling water for 15 minutes or until tender. Drain well and cool slightly. Heat the olive oil in a large saucepan over medium heat. Add the onion and garlic, and cook for 6–7 minutes, or until softened. Remove from the heat, add the potato and use a potato masher to mash into a coarse purée. Stir in the feta, allspice, mint, parsley and egg until well combined. Season with sea salt and freshly ground black pepper.

Preheat the oven to 180°C (350°F/Gas 4) and lightly grease a large baking tray. Lay the filo sheets on a clean work surface and cover with a damp tea towel (dish towel) to prevent them from drying out while you work. Take one sheet of filo pastry and brush with melted butter, then lay another sheet over the top and brush this lightly with butter. Cut the pastry into four even quarters. Working with one piece at a time, take 1 tablespoonful of the potato mixture and form into a neat log about 8 cm (3¼ inches) long. Place a log along the long edge of each pastry quarter, then roll up, folding in the ends as you roll, taking care not to roll too tightly or the pastry could burst while baking. Place the pastry rolls onto the prepared trays, seam side down. Repeat with the remaining filo and filling — you should make 28 rolls in total. Brush the tops of the rolls with the remaining melted butter and sprinkle generously with nigella seeds.

Bake in the oven for 20–30 minutes, or until light golden. Serve warm.

MAKES 28

URFA: WOOD-FIRED BREAD AND FAMOUS PEPPERS

When in public you could be forgiven for thinking that Turkey beats to a distinctly male-oriented drum and nowhere is this played out more clearly than in the many wood-fired bakeries scattered around the city of Urfa. These bakeries are a hub of activity, with their deep stone ovens and inviting aromas of freshly baked bread. Typically, a group of men stand in a line vigorously kneading, shaping and rolling dough into flat loaves, while others, sweaty from their exertions, work the inferno, removing baked loaves and depositing uncooked ones into the hot glowing coals using long wooden paddles. On any given morning customers, all male, drop by the bakeries with armfuls of eggplants and shiny red capsicums, which they deposit, along with their bread orders. They then return ten minutes later to pick up their steaming loaves and the vegetables, which have since been charred to crunchy perfection. This is breakfast in Urfa!

At lunch time I stand outside another *firin*, or communal oven, and watch as men and boys dash in with trays of food (typically a simple layered arrangement of meat and seasonal vegetables) before rushing off to midday prayers. About forty minutes later, they swing past to pick up the bread with their hot lunch. It's clearly a daily ritual, and one from which the women seem largely absent; when I do see women out and about they tend to be in the company of a male relative or another woman at least. Certainly not alone.

But there is another incentive for visiting this seductive city. All over Turkey, wherever you dine, food is offered with little paots or shakers of hot dried chilli flakes — the most celebrated of these come from Kahramanaras (also famed for its stretchy ice cream, known as dondurma) and from Urfa. The Urfa pepper is, in its most desirable form, an artisanal product. The peppers grow in the barren countryside around the city and, because they ripen at different rates, are all picked by hand. Many producers still dry them the ancient way, in the sun, then ferment them slightly afterwards. This gives the processed flakes their characteristic ox-blood colour and unmistakable flavour of earth and smoke. The taste is addictive and the sight and smell of them in the bazaars, heaped in great cones awaiting sale, is tantalising. And wholly unforgettable.

Simit is, for me, the quintessential Turkish food. To describe these round, chewy bread rings as 'sesame-encrusted bread' really isn't doing them justice; their flavour and deeply satisfying texture are quite unlike anything else. Turks eat simit daily, as a snack, but they really come into their own as fortifying breakfast fare, accompanied by cheese, tomatoes, cucumbers and olives.

SIMIT

METHOD

Combine the sugar and 60 ml (2 fl oz/$\frac{1}{4}$ cup) lukewarm water in a small bowl, then sprinkle over the yeast. Set aside for about 8 minutes, or until foamy, then add another 310 ml (10$\frac{3}{4}$ fl oz/1$\frac{1}{4}$ cups) lukewarm water.

Combine the flour and salt in a bowl, then add the yeast mixture and stir to form a coarse dough. Turn out onto a lightly floured surface and knead for 6–7 minutes, or until the dough is smooth and elastic. Roll the dough into a ball and place in a lightly oiled bowl, turning to coat. Cover with plastic wrap and set aside in a warm, draught-free place for 1 hour, or until doubled in size.

Preheat the oven to 220°C (425°F/Gas 7) and line two baking trays with baking paper. Knock back the dough on a lightly floured work surface and divide it into 10 even-sized pieces. Combine the pekmez with 80 ml (2$\frac{1}{2}$ fl oz/$\frac{1}{3}$ cup) water in a large bowl. Place the sesame seeds on a large plate. Working with one piece of dough at a time, use your hands to roll the dough out to make ten 55 cm (22 inch) long ropes. Fold in half so the two ends align, then lift off the board and use your hands to twist each rectangle into a two-stranded 'rope'. Place back on the work surface and join the ends together to make a circle, pressing the ends firmly together to seal. Repeat with the remaining dough to make 10 rope circles.

Dip each ring, first into the pekmez mixture, immersing completely to coat, then drain well and toss in the sesame seeds, turning gently to coat. Transfer to the prepared trays and set aside at room temperature for about 20 minutes, to puff slightly. Bake in the oven for 15–18 minutes, or until deep golden and cooked through. Transfer to a wire rack to cool. Simit are best eaten on the day of making but will keep, frozen in an airtight container, for up to 1 month. **MAKES 10**

Note: Pekmez is a molasses-like syrup made from the juice and must of certain fruits, usually grapes or figs. It is available from Middle Eastern and Turkish grocery stores.

INGREDIENTS

1 pinch sugar

3 teaspoons dried yeast

500 g (1 lb 2 oz/3$\frac{1}{3}$ cups) plain (all-purpose) flour

1$\frac{1}{2}$ teaspoons sea salt

170 ml (5$\frac{1}{2}$ fl oz/$\frac{2}{3}$ cup) pekmez (see note)

235 g (8$\frac{1}{2}$ oz/1$\frac{1}{2}$ cups) sesame seeds

LEEK AND BROAD BEAN BÖREK

INGREDIENTS

80 g (2¾ oz) butter, plus extra, for greasing

1.5 kg (3 lb 5 oz) leeks, trimmed, rinsed and finely sliced

1 kg (2 lb 4 oz) broad (fava) beans, podded

200 g (7 oz) grated kashkaval cheese (see note)

½ teaspoon freshly grated nutmeg

3 eggs

170 ml (5½ fl oz/⅔ cup) full-cream (whole) milk

DOUGH

400 g (14 oz/2⅔ cups) plain (all-purpose) flour

2 eggs, lightly beaten

2 tablespoons olive oil

1 tablespoon white vinegar

80 g (2¾ oz) Greek-style yoghurt

1 teaspoon salt

METHOD

To make the dough, place the flour in a bowl and make a well in the centre. In a separate bowl, combine the remaining ingredients with 60 ml (2 fl oz/¼ cup) water and whisk well to combine. Add to the flour, and gently combine to form a soft dough, adding an extra 1 tablespoon water if the dough is too stiff. Turn out onto a lightly floured work surface and knead for 3 minutes, or until smooth and elastic. Place in a lightly oiled bowl, cover with plastic wrap and stand at cool room temperature for 30 minutes.

Meanwhile, heat half the butter in a large saucepan over medium heat. Add the leek, cover, then reduce the heat to medium–low and cook for 25 minutes, stirring often until the leek is very soft. Drain in a colander and cool.

Cook the broad beans in salted boiling water for 5–6 minutes, drain well, then cool under running water. Drain again and peel and discard the tough outer skins. Combine the leek and cheese in a bowl. Lightly beat two of the eggs and add to the leek mixture. Stir in the broad beans and season with sea salt and freshly ground black pepper.

Melt the remaining butter and add to a separate bowl with the milk and remaining egg, stirring well to combine.

Grease the base and sides of two 20 cm (8 inch) round cake tins with butter. Divide the dough into eight even-sized portions. Roll each portion out on a lightly floured work surface to make a circle, about 2 mm (¹⁄₁₆ inch) thick, taking care the pastry does not tear. Line each tin with a pastry round, carefully easing it into the corners and allowing the excess to overhang. Brush the milk mixture generously over the pastry and add another layer of pastry to each tin. Brush with milk again and add another layer of pastry over the top — you should have three layers of pastry for each pie base. Divide the filling between both bases.

Cut both of the remaining dough portions in half again. Roll each half out into thin circles with a 20 cm (8 inch) diameter for the lids. Place over each pie and brush with the milk mixture. Place the remaining pastry over the top, creating two layers of pastry for each lid, and brush with the milk mixture. Bring any overhanging pastry up from the side, stretching them if necessary to pull them at least part-way over the top. Bake for 1 hour, or until the pastry is golden and cooked through. Serve warm or at room temperature. **SERVES 10–12**

Note: Kashkaval cheese is a semi-hard cheese that is popular throughout the Balkans as well as Turkey, where it is often made from sheep's milk.

BEETROOT LEAF, RICOTTA AND HAZELNUT GÖZLEME

METHOD

Combine the flour and salt in a large bowl and make a well in the centre. Add 250 ml (9 fl oz/1 cup) water and 2 tablespoons of the olive oil and stir with a flat-bladed knife, gradually incorporating more of the flour into the liquid as you go, until a coarse, soft dough forms. Turn out onto a lightly floured surface and knead for 5–6 minutes, or until smooth and elastic, adding a little extra flour if the dough is too sticky. (Take care not to add too much flour as the dough should be soft.) Roll the dough into a ball and place in a lightly oiled bowl, turning to coat. Cover with plastic wrap and set aside in a warm, draught-free place for 1 hour.

Meanwhile, heat the remaining oil in a saucepan over medium heat. Add the garlic and cook for 2 minutes, or until fragrant. Add the sultanas and beetroot leaves and stalks, cover the pan, and cook for 6 minutes, or until softened. Increase the heat to high, add the spinach and cook for 2–3 minutes, or until the spinach has wilted. Remove the green leaf mixture to a bowl using a slotted spoon, then continue to boil the pan juices for 3–4 minutes, or until reduced to about 2 tablespoons. Add to the leaf mixture in the bowl and cool to room temperature. Add the nutmeg, ricotta and hazelnuts, season with sea salt and freshly ground black pepper, then gently stir to just combine.

Divide the dough into 12 even-sized pieces. Working with one piece of dough at a time, roll each into a ball using your hands. Use a rolling pin to then roll into circles, each with a 21 cm (8¼ inch) diameter. Place 2 tablespoons of the filling on one side of each circle. Brush the edge of each circle lightly with the egg. Fold the dough over to make half-moon shapes and pinch to seal and enclose the filling. Place on the prepared trays, press down to flatten slightly, and sprinkle with extra flour.

Heat about 1 tablespoon of oil in a large, heavy-based frying pan over medium heat and cook the gözleme, in batches, for 4–5 minutes on each side, or until deep golden and the filling is heated through. Serve immediately.
MAKES 12

INGREDIENTS

300 g (10½ oz/2 cups) plain (all-purpose) flour, plus extra, for dusting

1 teaspoon salt

80 ml (2½ fl oz/⅓ cup) olive oil, plus extra, for cooking

3 garlic cloves, thinly sliced

60 g (2¼ oz/½ cup) sultanas (golden raisins)

leaves and stalks from 2 bunches beetroot, rinsed and chopped

350 g (12 oz) English spinach, rinsed and chopped

1 large pinch freshly grated nutmeg

250 g (9 oz/1 cup) crumbled firm ricotta cheese

100 g (3½ oz/¾ cup) hazelnuts, roasted, skinned and chopped

1 egg, lightly beaten

CAPPADOCIA AND A WISTFUL DREAM OF YUFKA DOUGH

Situated in the heart of Anatolia, the region of Cappadocia is famed worldwide for its singular landscapes and quirky vernacular architecture. The amazing 'fairy chimney' rock dwellings, hewn from cliff faces and rising dramatically out of the volcanic tuff, is part of the reason the area has such enormous historical significance. It has been settled for millennia, notably by the Hittites as far back as 2000BC and has an eerie atmosphere, unique to well-worn places that have seen humans come and go for a very long time. Persecuted early Christians took refuge in deep valleys, carving homes, churches and monasteries out of entire hills and high into rock walls. They left behind a veritable trove of Byzantine art, troglodyte villages and underground towns.

I stay in a guesthouse in Göreme, an admittedly pretty town, but one that has given over to tourism in such a way that it has arguably lost its soul. The guesthouse owner is an anthropologist who first visited from his native Germany some thirty years ago to study Cappadocian dwellings. In the relatively few decades since then, he's witnessed the complete disintegration of traditional life in the town and I find the subject fascinating. Back in the 1980s, he saw how local women would gather annually, several households together, to make enough sheets of yufka dough to last them through the year. They'd bury themselves deep in mixing, kneading and rolling the dough for days on end until the job was done. It was real secret women's business, he tells me. 'They didn't just make yufka — it was an important time for bonding, sorting out problems and differences, venting about husbands and imparting advice to the younger ones. It was part of what held the community together.'

Once made, the fragile yufka dough would keep in the dry, cool interiors of the traditional rock homes without spoiling, almost indefinitely. Today, this activity, like many other traditional, communal practices, has gone the way of the fez. People run internet cafés and bars for backpackers or get up early to bundle visitors into crammed hot-air balloon baskets — the 'essential' Cappadocian experience. They buy their yufka from the market. Despite this realisation I can't help but start fantasising about how the baked yufka dough, rolled into thin circular sheets and baked on hot iron plates, would taste. My mind runs riot with the many possible uses I could find for it.

HOMEMADE PASTA WITH ROCKET, FETA, WALNUTS AND HERBS

METHOD

To make the pasta, whisk the egg and milk in a bowl until well combined. Sift the flour and sea salt into a large bowl, stir in the semolina and make a well in the centre. Add the egg and milk mixture and stir with a fork to form a soft dough. Turn out onto a lightly floured surface and knead for 5 minutes, or until the dough is smooth and elastic. Roll the dough into a ball and place in a lightly oiled bowl, turning to coat. Cover with plastic wrap and set aside.

Turn the dough out onto a lightly floured surface and divide into two even-sized pieces. Working with one piece at a time, roll into a 60 x 40 cm (24 x 16 inch) rectangle, using a rolling pin. Cut each rectangle into thirds lengthways. Arrange the pasta sheets between layers of lightly floured tea towels (dish towels) and set aside at room temperature for 8 hours to dry slightly. Transfer to a board and cut each strip lengthways into 1 cm ($\frac{1}{2}$ inch) wide strips and dust lightly with flour.

Bring a large saucepan of salted water to the boil. Add the pasta and cook for 5–6 minutes, or until *al dente*. Drain well and set aside, reserving about 125 ml (4 fl oz/$\frac{1}{2}$ cup) of the cooking water.

Meanwhile, heat the olive oil in a large, deep frying pan or saucepan over medium heat. Add the garlic and walnuts and cook for 3 minutes, or until the garlic is fragrant. Add the rocket, parsley and dill and stir for 1–2 minutes, or until wilted. Add the cooked pasta and enough of the reserved cooking liquid to moisten the pasta. Add the feta and toss gently to combine. Divide the pasta among serving plates and serve immediately. **SERVES 4**

INGREDIENTS

100 ml ($3\frac{1}{2}$ fl oz) extra virgin olive oil

3 garlic cloves, finely chopped

120 g ($4\frac{1}{4}$ oz) chopped walnuts

1 bunch rocket (arugula), rinsed and coarsely chopped

1 bunch flat-leaf (Italian) parsley, chopped

1 bunch dill, chopped

200 g (7 oz/$1\frac{1}{3}$ cups) crumbled goat's feta cheese

ERISTE PASTA

2 eggs, lightly beaten

200 ml (7 fl oz) full-cream (whole) milk

400 g (14 oz/$2\frac{2}{3}$ cups) plain (all-purpose) flour, plus extra, for dusting

$1\frac{1}{2}$ teaspoons sea salt

60 g ($2\frac{1}{4}$ oz/$\frac{1}{2}$ cup) fine semolina

DILL, LEMON AND FETA POĞAÇA

INGREDIENTS

250 ml (9 fl oz/1 cup) full-cream (whole)
    milk
80 g (2¾ oz) butter
55 g (2 oz/¼ cup) caster (superfine) sugar
3 teaspoons dried yeast
1 egg, lightly beaten
¼ cup chopped dill
finely grated zest of 2 lemons
675 g (1 lb 8 oz/4½ cups) plain
    (all-purpose) flour
2½ teaspoons sea salt
200 g (7 oz) feta cheese, cubed

METHOD

Put the milk and butter in a small saucepan over low heat until the mixture is lukewarm. Remove from the heat and set aside.

Combine the sugar and 125 ml (4 fl oz/½ cup) lukewarm water in a small bowl, then sprinkle over the yeast. Set aside for about 8 minutes, or until foamy.

Combine the yeast and milk mixtures in a large bowl and add the egg, dill and lemon zest, stirring well to combine. Add 600 g (1 lb 5 oz/4 cups) of the flour and the salt, and stir to form a coarse dough. Add a little of the remaining flour if the dough is too wet — it should still be a little soft so take care not to add too much flour. Turn out onto a lightly floured surface and knead for 5–6 minutes, or until the dough is smooth and elastic. Roll the dough into a ball and place in a lightly oiled bowl, turning to coat. Cover with plastic wrap and set aside in a warm, draught-free place for 1 hour, or until doubled in size.

Preheat the oven to 180°C (350°F/Gas 4) and lightly grease two baking trays. Knock back the dough on a lightly floured surface and divide into 12 even-sized pieces. Use your hands to roll each piece into a ball. Flatten each ball into a disc and divide the cubed feta among the rounds. Bring the edges of each disc together to form balls again and enclose the feta, then roll over the work surface to neaten. Transfer to the prepared trays and cover loosely with a damp tea towel (dish towel), then set aside for 30 minutes or until risen slightly.

Bake in the oven for 20 minutes, or until golden and cooked through. Transfer to a wire rack to cool and serve at room temperature. Poğaça are best served on the day of making but will keep, frozen in an airtight container, for up to 1 month. **MAKES 12**

CHICKEN AND BLACK-EYED PEA MANTI

Put the black-eyed peas in a saucepan and add just enough water to cover, then bring to a boil. Reduce the heat to low and simmer for 35 minutes, or until tender. Drain well, reserving 250 ml (9 fl oz/1 cup) of the cooking liquid. Set aside.

To make the yufka dough, place the flour and salt in a large bowl and make a well in the centre. Combine the egg in a bowl with 125 ml (4 fl oz/$^1/_2$ cup) water and whisk well to combine. Add to the flour and use your hands to mix together, adding a little more water as needed to form a soft dough. Turn out onto a lightly floured surface and knead for 3 minutes, or until smooth and elastic. Place in a lightly oiled bowl, cover with plastic wrap and refrigerate for 30 minutes.

To make the filling, heat the olive oil in a large saucepan over medium heat. Add the onion and garlic and cook for 5 minutes, or until softened. Add the tomato paste, allspice and half the paprika, and stir for 1–2 minutes, or until fragrant. Add the chicken, tomato, reserved cooking liquid and oregano. Bring to a simmer and cook over low heat for 50 minutes, or until the chicken is very tender. Remove the chicken and when cool enough to handle, remove the meat, discarding the skin and bones. Shred the meat coarsely.

Skim any excess fat from the tomato mixture, add the peas and simmer for 10–15 minutes, or until reduced and thickened slightly. Remove the oregano sprigs and return the chicken meat to the pan. Season with sea salt and freshly ground black pepper, then cover the pan and continue cooking for a further 5–10 minutes, or until heated through.

Preheat the oven to 180°C (350°F/Gas 4) and lightly grease a large baking tray. Divide the dough into four even-sized pieces. Working with one piece of dough at a time, roll out on a lightly floured surface to a 36 x 22 cm (14$^1/_4$ x 8$^1/_2$ inch) rectangle, using a rolling pin. Cut each rectangle in half widthways, then cut strips, about 1.5 cm ($^5/_8$ inch) wide. Place these strips on the prepared trays and brush well with the melted butter. Bake in the oven, in batches, for 12–15 minutes, or until golden and crisp. When all the strips are baked, divide among shallow bowls then spoon the chicken mixture over.

Heat the remaining butter until foaming, then add the remaining paprika and the chilli flakes and drizzle over the chicken sauce. Sprinkle with the parsley and serve with the yoghurt passed separately. **SERVES 4**

135 g (4$^3/_4$ oz/$^2/_3$ cup) black-eyed peas, soaked overnight and drained

2 tablespoons extra virgin olive oil

1 onion, finely chopped

4 garlic cloves, crushed

2$^1/_2$ tablespoons tomato paste (concentrated purée)

1 teaspoon ground allspice

1 tablespoon sweet paprika

4 x 300 g (10$^1/_2$ oz) chicken leg quarters (marylands)

400 g (14 oz/1$^2/_3$ cups) tin chopped tomatoes

4 oregano sprigs

80 g (2$^3/_4$ oz) butter, melted, for brushing

1 teaspoon dried chilli flakes, or to taste

1 cup flat-leaf (Italian) parsley leaves, chopped

Greek-style yoghurt, to serve

YUFKA DOUGH

300 g (10$^1/_2$ oz/2 cups) plain (all-purpose) flour

$^1/_2$ teaspoon sea salt

2 eggs, lightly beaten

Although we often tend to think of it as a type of pizza or Turkish flat bread, pide is actually the general name given to several types of bread loaves served throughout Turkey. They are baked in high-temperature ovens, often fired by wood, and are crusty and chewy. While the authentic effect is hard to emulate at home, this version is simple to make and tastes fantastic.

PIDE

METHOD

Heat the milk and butter in a small saucepan over low heat until the mixture is lukewarm. Remove from the heat and set aside.

Combine the sugar and 125 ml (4 fl oz/$\frac{1}{2}$ cup) lukewarm water in a small bowl, then sprinkle over the yeast. Set aside for about 8 minutes, or until foamy.

Combine the yeast and milk mixtures in a large bowl and add the flour and salt, stirring to form a coarse dough. Turn out onto a lightly floured surface and knead for 6–7 minutes, or until the dough is smooth and elastic. Roll the dough into a ball and place in a lightly oiled bowl, turning to coat. Cover with plastic wrap and set aside in a warm, draught-free place for 1 hour, or until doubled in size.

Preheat the oven to 200°C (400°F/Gas 6) and lightly grease a large baking tray. Knock back the dough on a lightly floured work surface and divide it into equal halves. Roll each half into a round with a 22 cm (8$\frac{1}{2}$ inch) diameter, about 4 cm (1$\frac{1}{2}$ inches) thick, using a rolling pin. Cover loosely with a tea towel (dish towel) and stand at room temperature for 30 minutes, or until risen slightly.

Brush each round with milk and use a very sharp knife to cut shallow 4 cm (1$\frac{1}{2}$ inch) diamonds on top of the dough. Sprinkle with nigella or sesame seeds, then bake for 30–35 minutes, or until golden and cooked through. Turn out onto a wire rack to cool. **MAKES 2 LOAVES**

INGREDIENTS

1$\frac{1}{2}$ tablespoons caster (superfine) sugar

2 teaspoons dried yeast

250 ml (9 fl oz/1 cup) full-cream (whole) milk, plus extra, for brushing

60 g (2$\frac{1}{4}$ oz) butter

675 g (1 lb 8 oz/4$\frac{1}{2}$ cups) plain (all-purpose) flour

2 teaspoons sea salt

2 tablespoons nigella or sesame seeds

Manti are the ravioli of Anatolia. They are admittedly a little fiddly to make, as the dough needs to be rolled thinly and cut into fine squares, filled with a smidgeon of meat and sealed into neat little parcels. But the effort is well worth it — they taste delicious with yoghurt and a slick of herb and spice butter.

CLASSIC MANTI

INGREDIENTS

400 g (14 oz) minced (ground) lamb or beef
1 small onion, finely chopped
1 garlic clove, crushed
100 g (3½ oz) butter
2 teaspoons paprika
2 teaspoons dried mint
1 teaspoon dried chilli flakes, or to taste
500 g (1 lb 2 oz/2 cups) Greek-style yoghurt

YUFKA DOUGH

300 g (10½ oz/2 cups) plain
    (all-purpose) flour
1 teaspoon salt
2 eggs, lightly beaten

METHOD

To make the yufka dough, place the flour and salt in a large bowl and make a well in the centre. Combine the egg in a bowl with 125 ml (4 fl oz/½ cup) water and whisk well to combine. Add to the flour and use your hands to mix together, adding a little more water as needed to form a soft dough. Turn out onto a lightly floured work surface and knead for 3 minutes, or until smooth and elastic. Place in a lightly oiled bowl, cover with plastic wrap and refrigerate for 30 minutes.

To make the filling, combine the mince, onion and garlic in a bowl, season well with sea salt and freshly ground black pepper then, using your hands, mix until well combined and smooth.

Divide the dough into four even-sized portions and cover with a damp tea towel (dish towel) to prevent them from drying out. Line two baking trays with baking paper. Working with one portion of dough at a time, roll out on a lightly floured surface to create a large, paper-thin rectangle; the dough should be extremely thin. (Lightly flour the rolling pin to ensure the dough does not tear.) Using a large, sharp knife, neaten the edges of the rectangle, then cut into 4 cm (1½ inch) squares. Take ½ teaspoon of the filling at a time and roll into tiny balls. Place a meatball in the middle of each square. Lift up the four corners to join in the middle, pressing to seal and create a square parcel with seams running down each side. Place onto the prepared trays and cover. Repeat this process with the remaining dough and filling until it is all used.

Bring a large saucepan of salted water to the boil and cook the manti, in batches, for 4–5 minutes each, or until they rise to the surface and the filling is cooked through. Drain well and divide among warm serving bowls.

Melt the butter in a frying pan over medium–high heat until it sizzles, then add the paprika, dried mint and chilli flakes, and cook for 30 seconds or until the butter foams. Spoon the yoghurt over the manti, then drizzle over the butter and serve immediately. **SERVES 4**

VEGETABLES AND SALADS

As a food-producing country, Turkey wants for nothing; it's one of the few nations in the world that grows more than it needs to feed itself. In Turkey, eating according to the seasons and buying locally is commonplace. A stroll through a Turkish produce market is a joy — in late summer the tomatoes and capsicums are so ripe they're almost at bursting point, while in spring, artichokes, leeks and bunches of greens are fat and lush. The typical Turkish diet relies heavily on a variety of vegetables and these are prepared in such a way as to leave them tasting deeply and unforgettably of little but themselves.

PEKMEZ ROASTED PEAR, FETA, WATERCRESS AND HAZELNUT SALAD

METHOD

Preheat the oven to 180°C (350°F/Gas 4). Cut the unpeeled pears in half lengthways and remove the cores. Cut the halves into thirds lengthways, then place the pear wedges in a single layer in a small baking dish. Drizzle with the pekmez and olive oil and roast for about 30 minutes, turning once, until the pears are very tender and deep golden all over and the cooking juices are reduced and sticky. Remove from the oven and cool to room temperature.

Meanwhile, to make the dressing, combine the vinegar, garlic, pekmez and cumin in a small bowl and whisk well to combine. Whisking constantly, slowly add the olive oil in a thin stream, then season with sea salt and freshly ground black pepper.

Spread the watercress over a serving platter then scatter over the pear, cheese and hazelnuts. Drizzle the dressing over the top and serve. **SERVES 6**

INGREDIENTS

6 corella pears

1½ tablespoons pekmez (see note page 73)

1 tablespoon extra virgin olive oil

90 g (3¼ oz/3 cups) watercress

200 g (7 oz) feta cheese or goat's cheese, crumbled

70 g (2½ oz/½ cup) hazelnuts, roasted, peeled and chopped

DRESSING

2 tablespoons red wine vinegar

1 garlic clove, crushed

2 tablespoons pekmez

1 teaspoon cumin seeds, dry-roasted and crushed

125 ml (4 fl oz/½ cup) extra virgin olive oil

BORLOTTI BEAN PILAKI

INGREDIENTS

300 g (10½ oz/1½ cups) dried borlotti
(cranberry) beans, soaked overnight
and drained

80 ml (2½ fl oz/⅓ cup) olive oil

2 onions, chopped

3 garlic cloves, finely chopped

1 carrot, finely chopped

1 red capsicum (pepper), seeded, membrane
removed and finely chopped

2½ teaspoons sweet paprika

1½ tablespoons Turkish pepper paste
(see note page 13)

1 tablespoon caster (superfine) sugar

1 handful flat-leaf (Italian) parsley,
leaves chopped

extra virgin olive oil, to serve

METHOD

Put the borlotti beans in a saucepan and add just enough water to cover. Bring to a simmer and cook over medium heat for 30–40 minutes, or until just tender. Drain well.

Meanwhile, heat the olive oil in a large saucepan, add the onion, garlic, carrot and capsicum and cook, stirring, for 15 minutes, or until the vegetables are tender. Add the paprika and pepper paste and cook, stirring well, for another 2 minutes, then add the drained beans, sugar and enough cold water to just cover the beans. Simmer over low heat, uncovered, for 1–1½ hours, or until the beans are tender and the liquid has reduced — the beans should not be soupy. Season with sea salt and freshly ground black pepper, then remove from the heat and cool to room temperature. Stir in the parsley, then serve drizzled with a little extra virgin olive oil. **SERVES 6**

LONG-COOKED BEANS AND OKRA

INGREDIENTS

2½ tablespoons olive oil

1 onion, finely chopped

2 garlic cloves, crushed

350 g (12 oz) flat (Italian) beans, trimmed

350 g (12 oz) small okra, trimmed

2 teaspoons tomato paste
(concentrated purée)

800 g (1 lb 12 oz/3¼ cups) tin
chopped tomatoes

3 teaspoons sugar

dill sprigs, to serve

METHOD

Heat the olive oil in a large saucepan over medium heat. Add the onion and garlic and cook for 5–7 minutes, or until softened. Add the beans, okra and tomato paste and cook, stirring, for 2 minutes. Add the tomato and sugar, bring to a simmer, then reduce the heat to low, cover the pan, and cook for 10 minutes. Remove the lid and simmer the beans for a further 20 minutes, or until the liquid has reduced and the mixture has thickened. Remove from the heat and cool to room temperature. Season with sea salt and freshly ground black pepper and serve immediately with the dill as a garnish. **SERVES 6**

ZUCCHINI FRITTERS

Place the grated zucchini in a colander, sprinkle with the salt, toss to combine well then set aside for 20 minutes. Using your hands, squeeze the zucchini well to remove as much liquid as possible.

Heat 2 tablespoons of the olive oil in a large frying pan over medium heat. Add the onion and garlic and cook for 6–7 minutes, or until softened. Add the zucchini and cook, stirring, for another 4–5 minutes, or until the zucchini just starts to colour. Remove from the heat, transfer to a large bowl, and cool slightly. Add the flour, baking powder, egg, feta, parsley and dill and stir well to combine; season with sea salt and freshly ground black pepper.

Heat the remaining oil in a clean frying pan over medium heat, then cook heaped tablespoons of the zucchini mixture, in batches, for 3–4 minutes on each side, or until deep golden. Drain well on paper towels and serve immediately with the yoghurt. **MAKES ABOUT 16**

Variation: You can make these fritters with carrots instead of zucchini if you prefer — simply substitute the zucchini with 600 g (1 lb 5 oz) carrots — they need to be grated and squeezed dry in a clean tea towel (dish towel) before using. You can also add 100 g (3½ oz/¾ cup) coarsely chopped dried apricots to the mix or use kashkaval cheese instead of feta. If you opt for this variation you can omit the dill.

750 g (1 lb 10 oz) zucchini (courgettes), trimmed and coarsely grated

1½ teaspoons salt

125 ml (4 fl oz/½ cup) extra virgin olive oil

1 large onion, finely chopped

2 garlic cloves, finely chopped

110 g (3¾ oz/¾ cup) plain (all-purpose) flour, sifted

1 teaspoon baking powder

3 eggs, lightly beaten

225 g (8 oz/1½ cups) crumbled feta cheese

⅓ cup chopped flat-leaf (Italian) parsley

¼ cup chopped dill

Greek-style yoghurt, to serve

WILD GREENS IN AYVALIK

Even though I spend several months in Turkey, somehow I only manage to get to the coast once. An oversight really, as the country is bordered by no less than four seas — the Black, the Aegean, the Mediterranean and the Marmara. The coastal foray I do manage is to the pretty fishing village of Ayvalik on the north-west Aegean coast. For once I'm not solo, I've joined a tour. I hate group travel with a red-hot passion but as this is a Slow Food group from Istanbul, I figure the experience could be quite instructional.

The trip has been arranged so we can find out all about the wild greens harvest that happens here over the spring and summer months. All over the coast and in the hinterland, local women forage for a rich variety of plants that most of us would dismiss as weeds. There are dozens of types of edible wild greens here and people in these parts have long relied on them for a much-needed vitamin kick after a winter with little fresh produce. We stop for lunch at the home of one of the local olive oil producers and while we relax outside, we observe a local lady who is busy fossicking under some trees. Armed with just a small knife, she sweeps through the grass, regularly pausing to cut some green plant free and deposit it into a large bag. Within twenty minutes the bag is full of all manner of 'weeds' — there are dozens of varieties. She tells us she cooks them all separately, boiling them for fifteen minutes or so, and then dresses them with yoghurt or with garlic, lemon juice and olive oil to serve as a salad. They grow everywhere, she says, gesturing broadly around the area. I'm in awe of her abilities — everything growing underfoot looks unpromising to me.

Later, when we visit the Ayvalik market, the richness of this wild harvest falls into sharper focus. There are indeed dozens of types of these interesting greens for sale, piled high amid the more expected artichokes, leeks and carrots. There's wild fennel, wild mustard greens, mallow, samphire, wild chicory and nettles. There are wild radish greens, wild garlic, wild asparagus, various types of thistle, wild sorrel and dock. Some are used in salads while others, I'm told, are used for cooking in soups or incorporated into fillings for börek, omelettes or *bazlama*, a type of filled flat bread cooked on a griddle.

Wandering through these markets and sampling foods that I've never tasted before is simply one of my favourite things to do in the world. Even among complete strangers.

One of the most famous dishes in the extensive Turkish eggplant repertoire, the name of this dish literally means 'the imam fainted'. Supposedly he fainted on account of the expense of the ingredients (most likely the copious quantity of olive oil). They are great served as a meze.

IMAM BIYALDI

INGREDIENTS

1 kg (2 lb 4 oz) baby eggplants (aubergines)

250 ml (9 fl oz/1 cup) extra virgin olive oil

3 large onions, thinly sliced

3 garlic cloves, chopped

500 g (1 lb 2 oz) firm, ripe tomatoes

2 tablespoons chopped dill, plus extra, for serving

2 tablespoons chopped flat-leaf (Italian) parsley

60 ml (2 fl oz/¼ cup) freshly squeezed lemon juice

2½ teaspoons sugar

METHOD

Using a vegetable peeler, peel strips from the eggplant at 2 cm (¾ inch) intervals to give a striped effect. Cut a very deep slit along the length of each eggplant, taking care not to cut all the way through and leaving both ends intact. Submerge the eggplants in a large bowl of salted water, using a plate to keep them submerged, and stand for 20–30 minutes. Drain well and pat dry with paper towels.

Heat 2 tablespoons of the olive oil in a large saucepan over medium-low heat. Add the onion and garlic and cook for 7–8 minutes, or until softened. Remove from the heat and cool.

Cut a small cross in the base of each tomato and blanch them in a saucepan of boiling water for 1–2 minutes. Drain and plunge immediately into a bowl of cold water. Drain well, then peel and discard the skins and seeds, and finely chop the flesh. Combine with the onion mixture, dill and parsley in a bowl and season with sea salt and freshly ground black pepper.

Heat another 2 tablespoons of the oil in a large, deep frying pan over medium heat — the pan needs to be large enough to fit the eggplants in a single layer. Add the eggplants and cook for 7–8 minutes, turning often, until slightly softened. Remove the eggplants and cool.

Push the tomato and onion mixture into the slits in each eggplant so they are completely filled, then place the stuffed eggplant back into the frying pan. Scatter the remaining onion mixture over the top of the eggplants with the lemon juice, sugar and remaining oil. Add 60 ml (2 fl oz/¼ cup) water to the pan and bring to a simmer over low heat. Cover the pan with a tight-fitting lid and cook for 60–70 minutes, or until the eggplants are tender. Remove from the heat and cool to room temperature. To serve, scatter over the extra dill.
SERVES 6

TOPIK

METHOD

Cook the chickpeas in boiling salted water for 45 minutes, or until tender. Drain well, reserving 80 ml (2½ fl oz/⅓ cup) of the cooking liquid. When the chickpeas are cool, rub them vigorously in a clean tea towel (dish towel) to loosen the skins, removing as many as you can — this will improve the texture of the dish.

Combine the chickpeas, reserved cooking liquid and 80 ml (2½ fl oz/⅓ cup) of the olive oil in a food processor and pulse until smooth, scraping the sides a few times — you may need to do this in batches. Press the potatoes through a potato ricer or mash well and add to the chickpea mixture, using the pulse button to process until just combined. Season with sea salt and freshly ground black pepper and set aside.

Heat the remaining oil in a saucepan over medium heat. Add the onion and garlic and cook for 6–7 minutes, or until softened. Add the raisins, pistachios, spices and tahini and cook for 2 minutes, stirring well, until fragrant. Remove from the heat and cool, then season to taste and stir in the parsley.

Lightly grease the base and side of a loaf (bar) tin with oil. Place half of the chickpea mixture into the tin, pressing to form an even layer, then add all of the onion mixture to create a second layer. Smooth the remaining chickpea mixture on top. Cover in plastic wrap and refrigerate for at least 3 hours or overnight. To serve, turn the topik out of the mould and cut into slices. **SERVES 6–8**

INGREDIENTS

275 g (9¾ oz/1¼ cups) dried chickpeas, soaked overnight and drained

125 ml (4 fl oz/½ cup) extra virgin olive oil, plus extra, for greasing

350 g (12 oz) all-purpose potatoes, such as desiree, peeled, halved and boiled

2 onions, finely chopped

2 garlic cloves, crushed

40 g (1½ oz/⅓ cup) raisins, chopped

50 g (1¾ oz/⅓ cup) pistachios, chopped

½ teaspoon ground cinnamon

½ teaspoon ground allspice

2 tablespoons tahini

2½ tablespoons chopped flat-leaf (Italian) parsley

VINEGARED RAINBOW CHARD

METHOD

Cut the chard stems into 1 cm (½ inch) thick pieces. Tear the leaves into large pieces and set aside.

Heat the olive oil in a large saucepan over medium–low heat, add the chopped stems, garlic and cumin and cook for 5 minutes, or until softened. Increase the heat to medium–high, add the chard leaves and vinegar, cover the pan, and cook for 3–4 minutes, or until the leaves have wilted. Remove from the heat, strain off as much liquid as possible, set the vegetables aside and keep warm. Return the cooking juices to the pan and simmer for 4–5 minutes, or until the liquid has reduced. Place the chard in a bowl, season with sea salt and freshly ground black pepper. Serve warm or at room temperature with the reduced cooking liquid drizzled over the top. **SERVES 6–8**

INGREDIENTS

1.5 kg (3 lb 5 oz) rainbow chard, stalks trimmed, rinsed and dried

80 ml (2½ fl oz/⅓ cup) extra virgin olive oil

3 garlic cloves, thinly sliced

1 teaspoon cumin seeds

80 ml (2½ fl oz/⅓ cup) red wine vinegar

YOGHURT AND WALNUT-STUFFED EGGPLANT WITH TOMATO AND POMEGRANATE SAUCE

INGREDIENTS

900 g (2 lb/2 large) eggplants (aubergines)

1½ tablespoons salt

olive oil, for cooking

120 g (4¼ oz/2⅔ cups) baby spinach leaves

200 g (7 oz) goat's curd

250 g (9 oz/1 cup) Greek-style yoghurt

1 garlic clove, finely chopped

35 g (1¼ oz/⅓ cup) walnut halves,
    finely chopped

½ bunch flat-leaf (Italian) parsley,
    finely chopped

TOMATO AND POMEGRANATE SAUCE

1 kg (2 lb 4 oz) firm, ripe tomatoes

60 ml (2 fl oz/¼ cup) extra virgin olive oil

2 onions, finely chopped

3 garlic cloves, finely chopped

1½ tablespoons tomato paste
    (concentrated purée)

3 teaspoons caster (superfine) sugar

1 cinnamon stick

1 tablespoon pomegranate molasses (see note
    page 25)

METHOD

To make the sauce, cut a small cross in the base of each tomato and blanch them in a saucepan of boiling water for 1–2 minutes. Drain and plunge immediately into a bowl of cold water. Drain well, then peel and discard the skins and finely chop the flesh.

Heat the olive oil in a saucepan over medium heat. Add the onion and garlic and cook for 4–5 minutes, or until softened. Add the tomato paste and cook, stirring, for 1 minute, then add the tomato, sugar and cinnamon. Bring to a simmer, then reduce the heat to low and cook for about 30 minutes, or until the sauce has thickened. Remove from the heat and cool to room temperature. Remove the cinnamon stick and stir in the pomegranate molasses; season with sea salt and freshly ground black pepper. Set aside until ready to serve.

Cut the eggplants lengthways into 1.5 cm (⅝ inch) thick slices. Place the slices in layers in a large colander, sprinkling each layer lightly with salt. Stand over a sink for 30 minutes, then rinse well and pat dry with paper towels. Heat a chargrill plate or barbecue to medium. Brush the eggplant slices liberally with olive oil then cook, in batches, for 2–3 minutes on each side, or until charred and golden. Remove the cooked eggplant to a large plate and cool to room temperature.

Meanwhile, to make the filling, place the spinach leaves in a saucepan, cover with a tight-fitting lid and cook over medium–high heat for 2–3 minutes, or until just wilted. Transfer to a colander and cool to room temperature. Using your hands, press firmly on the spinach to remove as much excess liquid as possible. Finely chop the spinach and place in a bowl with the goat's curd, yoghurt, garlic, walnuts and parsley, stirring well to combine; season with sea salt and freshly ground black pepper.

Working with one eggplant slice at a time, place on a clean work surface with the short side facing you. Place a heaped tablespoon of the filling mixture in a thick line along one edge, then roll lengthways to form a neat roll. Repeat with the remaining eggplant slices and filling.

To serve, place the rolls on a serving platter and spoon the cooled sauce over the top. Serve immediately. The rolls can be made in advance, covered with plastic wrap and refrigerated for up to 6 hours and then sauced just before serving. Sauce can be made up to 2 days in advance; keep in an airtight container in the refrigerator and bring to room temperature before serving. **SERVES 6**

LENTIL, MINT AND FETA SALAD WITH POMEGRANATE DRESSING

To make the dressing, dry-fry the cumin seeds in a heavy-based frying pan over low heat, shaking the pan for 2 minutes, or until fragrant. Use a mortar and pestle to coarsely grind the cumin seeds, then combine in a bowl with the garlic, pomegranate molasses, sugar and chilli, whisking well to combine. Whisking constantly, add the olive oil in a slow, steady stream, then whisk in the lemon juice. Season with sea salt and freshly ground black pepper and set aside.

Put the lentils in a saucepan and add enough cold water to just cover. Bring to the boil, then reduce the heat to low, partially cover the pan, and cook the lentils for 25–30 minutes, or until just tender — take care not to overcook the lentils or they will be mushy. Drain well and cool to room temperature.

Meanwhile, heat a chargrill plate to medium. Cut the onions in half lengthways then cut each half into 5 mm ($\frac{1}{4}$ inch) thick wedges. Gently combine the onion with the oil, tossing well to coat. Cook the onions, in batches, for 3–4 minutes on each side, or until tender and lightly charred. Remove from the heat and cool.

Combine the cooled lentils, onion, walnuts, olives, parsley and mint in a large bowl and add the spinach leaves; season with sea salt and freshly ground black pepper. Toss gently to combine. Divide among serving bowls, top with the feta and drizzle the dressing over the top just before serving. **SERVES 4-6**

INGREDIENTS

325 g ($11\frac{1}{2}$ oz/$1\frac{3}{4}$ cups) brown or
    green lentils
2 red onions, peeled with root ends left intact
$2\frac{1}{2}$ tablespoons olive oil
50 g ($1\frac{3}{4}$ oz/$\frac{1}{2}$ cup) walnut halves,
    coarsely chopped
80 g ($2\frac{3}{4}$ oz/$\frac{1}{2}$ cup) pitted green olives, rinsed
1 handful flat-leaf (Italian) parsley, leaves
    chopped (optional)
1 cup mint leaves
100 g ($3\frac{1}{2}$ oz/$2\frac{1}{4}$ cups) baby spinach leaves
200 g (7 oz) feta cheese

POMEGRANATE DRESSING

1 teaspoon cumin seeds
2 garlic cloves, very finely chopped
1 tablespoon pomegranate molasses (see note
    page 25)
$\frac{1}{2}$ teaspoon caster (superfine) sugar
1 large pinch dried chilli flakes
125 ml (4 fl oz/$\frac{1}{2}$ cup) extra virgin olive oil
2 teaspoons freshly squeezed lemon juice

This is a typical example of a Turkish vegetable dish, which uses a copious quantity of olive oil to intensify the divine flavours of the main vegetable components and fresh herbs. It is best served at room temperature.

ARTICHOKES, CELERIAC AND CARROTS IN OLIVE OIL

METHOD

Strip the tough outer leaves from the artichokes, then using a sharp knife, cut off the top of each artichoke, right down to the top of the heart. Carefully trim back the outer layers of each artichoke to expose the heart. Using a teaspoon, scrape out the hairy choke. Place the prepared artichokes into a bowl of acidulated water (see note).

Bring a saucepan of salted water to the boil. Add 2 tablespoons of the lemon juice and the flour, stirring well, then add the artichoke and onions, reserving the acidulated water in the bowl. Cover the pan and simmer for 5 minutes, then drain well.

Peel the celeriac and cut into 2 cm ($^3/_4$ inch) pieces, placing them into the reserved acidulated water.

Place all the vegetables in a large saucepan. Add the stock, olive oil, sugar, thyme, bay leaf and 60 ml (2 fl oz/$^1/_4$ cup) of the lemon juice. Place a piece of baking paper over the vegetables to cover, then cover the pan with a lid. Bring to a simmer and cook over low heat for 30 minutes, or until the vegetables are very tender. Cool to room temperature in the liquid.

Transfer to a serving dish, season with sea salt and freshly ground black pepper, and a little extra lemon juice, if needed. **SERVES 6**

Note: Acidulated water is made by squeezing the juice of 1 lemon into a large bowl of water. It is used to help prevent certain fruits and vegetables from turning brown before cooking.

INGREDIENTS

8 globe artichokes, stems trimmed to 3 cm (1$^1/_4$ inch) from base of artichoke

125 ml (4 fl oz/$^1/_2$ cup) freshly squeezed lemon juice

3 teaspoons plain (all-purpose) flour

8 pickling onions, peeled, leaving root end intact, then halved

700 g (1 lb 9 oz) celeriac

500 g (1 lb 2 oz) purple Dutch carrots, trimmed and halved lengthways

300 ml (10$^1/_2$ fl oz) chicken stock

250 ml (9 fl oz/1 cup) extra virgin olive oil

2$^1/_2$ teaspoons caster (superfine) sugar

3 thyme sprigs

1 fresh bay leaf

TURLUTURLU

165 g (5¾ oz/¾ cup) dried chickpeas, soaked
    overnight and drained

400 g (14 oz/1 large) eggplant (aubergine),
    trimmed and cut into 4 cm (1½ inch)
    pieces

125 ml (4 fl oz/½ cup) extra virgin olive oil

3 garlic cloves, chopped

2 teaspoons ground coriander

2 teaspoons ground cumin

1 teaspoon dried chilli flakes, or to taste

1½ tablespoons sugar

2 red onions, cut into 3 cm (1¼ inch) pieces

400 g (14 oz) all-purpose potatoes, such as
    desiree, cut into 3 cm (1¼ inch) pieces

1 large red capsicum (pepper), seeded,
    membrane removed and cut into 4 cm
    (1½ inch) pieces

650 g (1 lb 7 oz) jap pumpkin (winter squash),
    peeled, seeded and cut into 3 cm
    (1¼ inch) pieces

3 zucchini (courgettes), trimmed, halved
    lengthways and cut into 4 cm
    (1½ inch) pieces

500 ml (17 fl oz/2 cups) tomato passata
    (puréed tomatoes)

1 cup coriander (cilantro) leaves, chopped

Cook the chickpeas in boiling salted water for 45 minutes, or until tender. Drain well.

Put the eggplant in a colander, sprinkling lightly with salt, and set aside for 30 minutes to drain. Rinse well, then pat dry on paper towels.

Preheat the oven to 180°C (350°F/Gas 4). Combine the olive oil, garlic, coriander, cumin, chilli and sugar in a large bowl and whisk well to combine. Add the eggplant, onion, potato and capsicum to the bowl and toss to coat. Divide the mixture between two baking dishes, spreading evenly over the base and drizzling over any oil left in the bowl. Cook for 35 minutes, then add the pumpkin and zucchini and cook for another 25 minutes, or until the vegetables are very tender and some are starting to char slightly. Scatter over the chickpeas, pour over the tomato passata, and continue cooking for 5–10 minutes, or until heated through. Scatter with the coriander and serve hot, warm or at room temperature. **SERVES 6**

TAKING TEA ON CUNDA ISLAND

I'm in Ayvalik, a seaside town on the Aegean coast, when I decide to take a short break from the tour group I've been with for the past few days. I decide to spend the morning at the market in Ayvalik sampling cheese, then I'm going to steal away to Cunda Island for some afternoon respite.

Before I head out of town I learn that Ayvalik cheeses are legendarily good and one of our group, a high-profile chef with a restaurant in the posh Istanbul suburb of Nişantasi, stocks up for her menu. I love the köy peynir, a young cow's milk cheese with a delicate, slightly flowery taste. My favourite quickly becomes *Lor peynir*, somewhat similar to ricotta but (dare I say this?) even better. It is a highly perishable fresh cheese that doesn't transport well and as a result is hard to find outside the area. It's creamy and rich and unbelievably smooth. I eat it as a light finish to lunch, served simply with homemade cherry jam and pekmez.

It's a kind of dessert that keeps me perfectly satisfied as I make my way to the slim causeway that joins the mainland near Ayvalik to Cunda Island. This is an idyllic spot that I soon learn, in season, is heaving with visitors — its minuscule population of two thousand triples during summer. I spend a blissful afternoon alone on Cunda, meandering up its winding old backstreets, where women sit knitting on stoops and kids kick balls against the walls of quaint old pastel-hued homes. From the hill that looms over the town there are views across the sea to Ayvalik and beyond. The waterfront promenade, packed with eateries, looks like the perfect spot for downing a raki or three and dining on seafood meze.

It's late in the afternoon and I venture into the Taş Kahve, a thoughtfully restored, 150-year-old tea house. The spacious interior features a high ceiling and lovely coloured glass windows. This is a male domain where tea drinking, card playing and newspaper reading are the activities of choice. I love the way no one particularly cares if I'm here, so I can sip my tea in peace and people-watch. In my coat pocket I happily find a couple of cookies I'd forgotten were there — special mastic-flavoured ones from a famous bakery in Ayvalik, made using olive oil and encrusted with sesame seeds. They're a regional speciality and are not too sweet; the perfect foil for the sugary tea. For a nanosecond I forget I'm expected back for dinner with the tour group. Right now I'm having a 'Turkey moment': taking tea in some atmospheric old pile and eating something I've never seen before, even if it is something as simple as a biscuit.

WHITE BEAN SALAD WITH TAHINI DRESSING AND GRILLED PRAWNS

INGREDIENTS

400 g (14 oz/2 cups) dried white beans,
    soaked overnight and drained
1 small red onion, very finely sliced
60 g (2¼ oz/½ cup) pitted green olives
1 cup flat-leaf (Italian) parsley leaves
2 tomatoes, cut into thin wedges
4 hard-boiled eggs, peeled and cut
    into quarters
36 raw king prawns (shrimp), peeled
    and deveined, tails left intact
olive oil, for cooking

DRESSING

2 garlic cloves, crushed
60 ml (2 fl oz/¼ cup) tahini
60 ml (2 fl oz/¼ cup) freshly squeezed
    lemon juice
finely grated zest of 1 lemon
125 ml (4 fl oz/½ cup) extra virgin olive oil
1 large pinch dried chilli flakes, or to
    taste (optional)

METHOD

Soak twelve wooden skewers in water for 30 minutes.

Put the beans in a saucepan and add just enough water to cover. Bring to a simmer and cook over medium–low heat for 50–60 minutes, or until very tender. Drain well and cool to room temperature.

Meanwhile, to make the dressing, combine the garlic, tahini, lemon juice and lemon zest in a bowl. Whisking constantly, slowly add the olive oil in a thin stream, then stir in 60 ml (2 fl oz/¼ cup) warm water until the dressing is a thick, creamy consistency. Season with sea salt, freshly ground black pepper and the chilli, to taste, then cover with plastic wrap and set aside.

Heat a chargrill or barbecue grill to medium. Combine the beans and the dressing in a large bowl and toss well to coat. Add the onion, olives, parsley, tomato and egg and toss very gently to just combine.

Thread the prawns onto skewers and brush all over with olive oil. Season well, then grill for about 4 minutes, turning once, until just cooked through. Divide the salad and prawn skewers among serving plates and serve immediately.
SERVES 6

VEGETABLES WITH BARLEY AND SPICED YOGHURT

To make the spiced yoghurt, heat the olive oil in a small saucepan over medium–low heat. Add the cumin and paprika and cook, stirring constantly, for 1–2 minutes, or until fragrant. Remove from the heat, transfer to a small bowl and cool to room temperature. Stir in the yoghurt, freshly ground black pepper and sea salt. Cover with plastic wrap and refrigerate until needed.

Cook the barley in a saucepan of simmering water for 30 minutes, or until tender. Drain well and cool to room temperature. Meanwhile, heat the oil in a large saucepan over medium–low heat. Add the onion, garlic and cinnamon and cook, for 4–5 minutes, or until softened. Add the carrot and celery and cook for 6–7 minutes, stirring regularly, until the vegetables have started to soften. Add the pepper paste and cook, stirring for 1 minute, then add the stock and bring to a simmer. Cover the pan and cook over medium–low heat for 10 minutes, or until the vegetables are very soft. Remove the cinnamon stick and discard.

Add the spinach, rocket, parsley and barley to the pan, stirring well to combine, then cover and cook for 3–4 minutes further, or until the greens have wilted. Remove from the heat and cool to room temperature. Season with sea salt and freshly ground black pepper. Transfer to a large serving dish and serve the barley and vegetables with the spiced yoghurt. **SERVES 6**

INGREDIENTS

220 g ($7^3/_4$ oz/1 cup) pearl barley

60 ml (2 fl oz/$^1/_4$ cup) extra virgin olive oil

1 onion, finely chopped

2 garlic cloves, finely chopped

1 cinnamon stick

2 carrots, finely sliced

2 celery sticks, finely chopped

1 tablespoon Turkish pepper paste (see note page 13)

250 ml (9 fl oz/1 cup) chicken stock

1 bunch spinach, stems trimmed, leaves rinsed, dried and coarsely chopped

1 bunch rocket (arugula), leaves rinsed, dried and coarsely chopped

1 cup flat-leaf (Italian) parsley leaves, chopped

SPICED YOGHURT

$1^1/_2$ tablespoons extra virgin olive oil

2 teaspoons cumin seeds

2 teaspoons sweet paprika

$^1/_2$ teaspoon dried chilli flakes, or to taste

500 g (1 lb 2 oz/2 cups) sheep's milk yoghurt

$^1/_2$ teaspoon freshly ground black pepper

1 teaspoon sea salt, or to taste

TOMATO, POMEGRANATE AND MINT SALAD WITH SAFFRON LABNEH

INGREDIENTS

1 pinch saffron threads

500 g (17 lb 2 oz/2 cups) Greek-style yoghurt

1 kg (2 lb 4 oz) mixed tomatoes

1 pomegranate, seeds removed

1/4 cup mint leaves

2 1/2 teaspoons sugar

2 tablespoons freshly squeezed lemon juice

60 ml (2 fl oz/1/4 cup) extra virgin olive oil

METHOD

Stir the saffron into the yoghurt, then spoon this mixture into a muslin (cheesecloth)-lined sieve placed over a bowl. Place the yoghurt in the refrigerator overnight to drain and thicken.

Cut the tomatoes into a variety of shapes — the larger ones into rounds, any egg tomatoes into wedges and the cherry and grape tomatoes into quarters. Arrange half of the tomatoes on a large platter, scatter over half of the sugar, season with sea salt and freshly ground black pepper, then scatter over half of the pomegranate seeds and mint leaves. Repeat with the remaining tomatoes, sugar, pomegranate and mint. Drizzle over the lemon juice and olive oil. Serve the salad with the yoghurt mixture on the side. **SERVES 6**

GREEN TOMATO PICKLE

INGREDIENTS

500 ml (17 fl oz/2 cups) white wine vinegar

2 garlic cloves, bruised

1 cinnamon stick

2 fresh bay leaves

2 teaspoons whole allspice berries

55 g (2 oz/¼ cup) caster (superfine) sugar

1½ tablespoons sea salt

800 g (1 lb 12 oz) green (unripe) tomatoes, cut into 1 cm (½ inch) wedges

METHOD

Combine the vinegar, garlic, cinnamon, bay leaves, allspice, sugar and salt in a saucepan with 250 ml (9 fl oz/1 cup) water. Bring to a simmer, stirring regularly, until the sugar and salt have dissolved. Place all of the tomato wedges in a 1.5 litre (52 fl oz/6 cup) capacity sterilised airtight jar and pour the mixture over the top to submerge the tomatoes — they should be just covered. Cool to room temperature then seal the jar. Refrigerate for about 8 weeks before using. Green tomato pickle can be stored for 2–3 months in the refrigerator once opened. **MAKES 1.5 litres (52 fl oz/6 cups)**

STUFFED EGGPLANT PICKLE

INGREDIENTS

1.2 kg (2 lb 10 oz) baby eggplants (aubergines)

6 garlic cloves, bruised

1 bunch dill

2 teaspoons whole coriander seeds, crushed

600 ml (21 fl oz) red wine vinegar

55 g (2 oz/¼ cup) sugar

2 tablespoons salt

METHOD

Bring a saucepan of water to a simmer, add the eggplants and cook over medium–low heat for 6 minutes, or until softened. Drain well and set aside. Once cool, use a sharp knife to cut the eggplants lengthways, leaving the stem end intact.

Combine the garlic, dill and coriander seeds in a bowl, then press into the cuts in each eggplant. Place the stuffed eggplants in a 1.5 litre (52 fl oz/6 cup) capacity sterilised airtight jar.

Mix together the vinegar, sugar and salt. Pour the vinegar mixture over the eggplants in the jar, seal, and set aside at room temperature for at least 3 weeks before using. Stuffed eggplant pickle can be stored for up to 3 months in the refrigerator once opened. **MAKES 1.5 litres (52 fl oz/6 cups)**

BEETROOT PICKLES IN CHERRY VINEGAR

METHOD

Cook the whole beetroots in boiling water for 30 minutes, or until tender. Drain well and cool slightly. When cool enough to handle, remove the beetroot skins and cut into halves. Place in a 1.25 litre (44 fl oz/5 cup) capacity sterilised airtight jar.

Combine the cinnamon, cloves, garlic, vinegar, sugar and salt in a saucepan with 375 ml (13 fl oz/1½ cups) water and bring to a simmer. Reduce the heat to low and cook for 6 minutes, stirring regularly. Pour the hot liquid over the beetroot in the jar and seal once cool. Keep in a cool dark place or in the refrigerator for at least 2 weeks before using. Beetroot pickles in cherry vinegar can be stored for 2–3 months in the refrigerator once opened. **MAKES 1.5 litres (52 fl oz/6 cups)**

INGREDIENTS

1.5 kg (3 lb 5 oz) baby beetroot (beets), trimmed and rinsed

2 cinnamon sticks, broken

2 teaspoons whole cloves

6 garlic cloves, bruised

500 ml (17 fl oz/2 cups) cherry vinegar

145 g (5 oz/⅔ cup) caster (superfine) sugar

2 tablespoons salt

LEMON CARROT PICKLE

METHOD

Cook the carrot and lemon peel in a saucepan of salted boiling water for 2 minutes, then drain well. Place the carrot and lemon peel into a 1.25 litre (44 fl oz/5 cup) capacity sterilised airtight jar with the thyme.

Meanwhile combine the garlic, coriander seeds, lemon juice, vinegar, honey and 375 ml (13 fl oz/1½ cups) water in a saucepan and bring to the boil. Simmer over low heat for 3–4 minutes, then pour over the carrots in the jar and seal once cool. Stand in a cool dark place or in the refrigerator for at least 1 week before using. Lemon carrot pickle can be stored for 2–3 months in the refrigerator once opened. **MAKES 1.5 litres (52 fl oz/6 cups)**

INGREDIENTS

1 kg (2 lb 4 oz) yellow and orange Dutch carrots, trimmed, peeled and halved lengthways

2 lemons, peel removed in 1 cm (½ inch) wide strips, white pith removed

6 thyme sprigs

4 garlic cloves, bruised

1½ teaspoons coriander seeds

185 ml (6 fl oz/¾ cup) freshly squeezed lemon juice

185 ml (6 fl oz/¾ cup) white vinegar

115 g (4 oz/⅓ cup) honey

RICE AND BURGHUL

Turkish rice is a variety called baldo and much of it is grown in north central Anatolia in and around Tosya. Grains are fat, somewhat like Italian arborio and are used in various types of dolma (stuffed dishes) and in pilafs. Turkish cooks pride themselves on their ability to cook rice well — the grains should still be somewhat firm and separate, never sticky or clumped together. It is this pride in cooking simple things very, very well that exemplifies the spirit of the Turkish kitchen. Likewise, burghul has had an important place on the table in Turkey since ancient times and is also fashioned into pilafs and salads.

PERDE PILAV

To make the dough, sift the flour and salt into a bowl. In a separate bowl, combine the egg, yoghurt, milk and olive oil and whisk until well combined. Add to the flour and stir to form a coarse dough. Turn the dough out onto a lightly floured surface and knead for 5 minutes, or until smooth, adding a little extra flour if the dough is too sticky. Roll the dough into a ball and place in a lightly oiled bowl, turning to coat. Cover with plastic wrap and set aside for 1 hour.

Meanwhile, coarsely chop one of the onions and place in a large saucepan with the chicken, carrot, celery and bay leaf. Add enough water to just cover the chicken, then cover the pan with a lid and slowly bring to a simmer over medium–low heat. Reduce the heat to very low and cook the chicken for 45 minutes, or until tender. Remove the chicken from the pan, then strain and reserve 750 ml (26 fl oz/3 cups) of the stock, discarding the solids. Remove the meat from the chicken, discarding the skin and bones. Finely shred the meat using your hands and set aside.

Melt the butter in a large saucepan over medium heat. Chop the remaining onion and add to the pan with the chopped almonds and pine nuts and cook for 7–8 minutes, or until the onion has softened and the nuts are light golden. Add the rice, currants and allspice and cook, stirring, for 2–3 minutes, or until the rice is well coated and the mixture is fragrant. Add the reserved stock, bring to a simmer, then cover with a tight-fitting lid and cook over low heat for about 10–12 minutes, or until almost all the liquid has been absorbed — the rice will not be quite cooked through. Remove from the heat, stir in the dill and chicken, and season with sea salt and freshly ground black pepper. Set aside to cool.

Preheat the oven to 180°C (350°F/Gas 4) and grease six 400 ml (14 fl oz) capacity pie tins or ovenproof dishes. Place 3 of the extra whole almonds in the base of each. Divide the pastry into 6 even-sized pieces and roll out on a lightly floured surface to make circles big enough to line the tins, about 1 cm (1/2 inch) thick. Use the pastry to line the tins, allowing any excess to overhang the edges — you will need to be careful not to tear the pastry as it is delicate. Spoon the rice mixture into the tins and fold over the excess pastry to cover the rice, pinching to seal. Bake in the oven for 50 minutes, or until the pastry is deep golden. Remove from the oven and cool in the tins for 5 minutes, then turn out and serve immediately with a green salad passed separately. **SERVES 6**

2 onions

1.2 kg (2 lb 10 oz) whole free-range chicken

1 carrot, chopped

1 celery stick, chopped

1 bay leaf

50 g (1¾ oz) butter, plus extra, for greasing

115 g (4 oz/¾ cup) blanched almonds, chopped, plus 18 whole almonds extra

50 g (1¾ oz/⅓ cup) pine nuts

400 g (14 oz/2 cups) long-grain white rice, rinsed and drained

100 g (3½ oz/⅔ cup) currants, soaked in hot water for 30 minutes and drained

2 teaspoons ground allspice

1 bunch dill, chopped

DOUGH

325 g (11½ oz) plain (all-purpose) flour

1 teaspoon

1 egg, lightly beaten

125 g (4½ oz/½ cup) Greek-style yoghurt

80 ml (2½ fl oz/⅓ cup) full-cream (whole) milk

60 ml (2 fl oz/¼ cup) olive oil

BURGHUL KÖFTE WITH TOMATO AND MINT SAUCE AND GARLIC YOGHURT

350 g (12 oz/2 cups) fine burghul (bulgur)

30 g (1 oz/¼ cup) fine semolina

50 g (1¾ oz/⅓ cup) plain (all-purpose) flour

1½ teaspoons ground cumin

1½ tablespoons Turkish pepper paste
   (see note page 13)

1½ teaspoons sea salt

1½ teaspoons freshly ground black pepper

TOMATO AND MINT SAUCE

60 ml (2 fl oz/¼ cup) extra virgin olive oil

1 large onion, finely chopped

3 garlic cloves, crushed

1½ teaspoons sweet paprika

1½ teaspoons dried mint

2 tablespoons tomato paste
   (concentrated purée)

1½ tablespoons Turkish pepper paste

750 ml (26 fl oz/3 cups) chicken or
   vegetable stock

2½ tablespoons freshly squeezed lemon
   juice, or to taste

GARLIC YOGHURT

375 g (13 oz/1½ cups) Greek-style yoghurt

2–3 garlic cloves, crushed

METHOD

To make the garlic yoghurt, combine the yoghurt and garlic in a bowl, season with sea salt and freshly ground black pepper and stir well to combine. Cover with plastic wrap and refrigerate until needed.

To make the tomato and mint sauce, heat the olive oil in a saucepan over medium–low heat. Add the onion and garlic and cook for 5–6 minutes, or until softened. Add the paprika, mint, tomato paste and pepper paste and cook for 2–3 minutes, stirring until fragrant. Add the stock and bring to a simmer, then reduce the heat to low, cover and cook for 5–6 minutes, stirring occasionally until smooth and thickened slightly. Stir in the lemon juice and season, to taste.

To make the burghul köfte, put the burghul in the bowl of an electric mixer fitted with a beater attachment. Add 250 ml (9 fl oz/1 cup) lukewarm water. Leave to soak for 5–6 minutes, or until all of the water has been absorbed. Add the semolina, flour, cumin, pepper paste, sea salt and pepper. Beat the mixture slowly, while gradually adding another 250 ml (9 fl oz/1 cup) water. Continue to beat slowly until soft and well combined. (Alternatively, you can mix the köfte in a large bowl and knead using your hands for 10–12 minutes until elastic.) Taking a heaped teaspoon of the mixture at a time, form into small balls, then use the tip of your little finger to make a small indentation in each ball.

Cook the köfte in a large saucepan of salted boiling water for 3–4 minutes, or until cooked through, then remove with a slotted spoon and keep warm while cooking the remaining köfte. Divide between serving dishes, spoon over the tomato and mint sauce and serve immediately with the garlic yoghurt passed separately. **SERVES 4–6**

ICLI KÖFTE

To make the filling, heat the olive oil in a frying pan over medium heat. Add the onion, lamb, garlic and walnuts and cook for about 15 minutes, breaking up the meat, until the liquid has evaporated and the meat is browned. Stir in the raisins and allspice, and cook for 1 minute, then remove to a bowl and cool. Season with sea salt and freshly ground black pepper, then set aside.

Preheat the oven to 200°C (400°F/Gas 6). Place the burghul in a bowl and add just enough cold water to cover, then set aside for 10 minutes. Drain well in a fine sieve, pressing down with your hands to remove as much liquid as possible.

Combine the burghul, lamb and onion in a food processor and process until well combined. Season to taste, then continue to process until the mixture feels elastic. Place a bowl of cold water on the work surface to wet your hands — this will prevent the mixture sticking to your hands as you work. With damp hands, take a heaped tablespoon of the mixture at a time and roll into a ball. Use your thumb to make an indentation deep into the ball, then use your hands to work the ball into a tall cup shape, making the sides as even and thin as you can without breaking them. Place 2 teaspoons of the filling mixture into the cavity of each, then close the burghul mixture around the filling, forming a torpedo-shaped kibbeh. Repeat with the remaining burghul mixture and filling — you should make about 20 in total.

Drizzle the oil over the base of a large baking dish, then arrange the kibbeh in a single layer in the base. Bake in the oven for 15 minutes, then turn the kibbeh over and bake for a further 10–15 minutes, or until golden and cooked through. Serve hot, warm or at room temperature with a green salad. **SERVES 6**

INGREDIENTS

235 g (8½ oz/1⅓ cups) fine burghul (bulgur)

400 g (14 oz) minced (ground) lamb

2 tablespoons grated onion

60 ml (2 fl oz/¼ cup) olive oil, for cooking

FILLING

1½ tablespoons olive oil

1 onion, finely chopped

250 g (9 oz) minced (ground) lamb

2 garlic cloves, finely chopped

25 g (1 oz/¼ cup) walnuts, chopped

30 g (1 oz/¼ cup) raisins, chopped

½ teaspoon ground allspice

STREET LIFE IN DIYARBAKIR

I knew I'd love Diyarbakir even before I saw it for the first time. It's an ancient city with a five-thousand-year history of continuous habitation. It lies on the edge of the great, fertile Mesopotamian Plain to the country's south-east, right near the mighty Tigris River. Its historic old centre is hemmed in by some six kilometres of brooding, basalt defensive walls.

The vernacular you hear on the streets of Diyarbakir is more likely to be Kurmanci than Turkish, and Kurdish cultural and intellectual activities are very much alive and kicking in the core of the city, which comprises a tight warren of ancient alleyways, complete with old mosques, churches and an energetic street life. There's some domestic tourism, but many Turks are anxious to avoid the place, as it was the scene of bloody tension between the outlawed PKK (Kurdistan Workers' Party) and the Turkish armed forces in the latter part of the 1990s — in fact, emergency rule was only lifted in the city in 2002. In the surrounding countryside, there's still a heavy army presence.

Compared to the slicker, more wealthy parts of Turkey, Diyarbakir, still has a raw, in-your-face immediacy. Nowhere is this more profoundly expressed than in the food. Here, things aren't so sanitised. Yoghurt is delivered to shops in big metal buckets, often left uncovered. Women congregate in narrow streets and roast whole eggplants over little wood fires that fill the neighbourhood with smoke. From a wall-top vantage point, I can look over the city in the late summer and see big tubs of capsicum purée evaporating slowly into a dense, rich paste in the blazing heat. The streets are a crush of humanity and the alleyways are the domain of children. Flat-roofed houses are festooned with strings of chillies and tomatoes drying in the sun to make ready for wintertime use. At the famed cheese market, big fat lengths of the local plaited cheese lie in briny baths, exposed to the ambient temperature.

On one corner a man stands all day, mixing tubs of ciğ köfte using his bare hands. Once cooked, he spreads the mince over squares of flat bread, scatters over some herbs and radishes and drenches it in pomegranate molasses, selling it, rolled neatly in yesterday's newspaper, for a few Turkish lira. Elsewhere, men fan kebab stands into life and young boys sell frothy copper cups of cold *ayran* to parched passers-by. Legions of men lounge in the afternoon sun drinking tea and smoking, while young simit sellers weave in and out, dispensing their wares to the hungry.

PUMPKIN TRAY KÖFTE

Preheat the oven to 180°C (350°F/Gas 4). To make the oregano–paprika roast tomatoes, put the tomatoes in a single layer in the base of a roasting dish and sprinkle over the sugar, spices and oregano leaves. Drizzle the olive oil and vinegar over the top, season with sea salt and freshly ground black pepper and cook for 1 hour, or until the tomatoes are soft and slightly charred around the edges.

To make the filling, heat the olive oil in a large frying pan over medium–high heat. Add the lamb, onion and garlic and cook for 7–8 minutes, stirring often to break up the meat. Add the tomato paste, allspice, cinnamon and chilli and cook, stirring, for another 2 minutes. Remove from the heat and stir in the chopped walnuts and parsley, then set aside to cool.

Place the burghul in a bowl and add just enough cold water to cover, then leave to soak for 10 minutes. Drain well in a fine sieve, pressing with your hands to remove as much liquid as possible.

Heat 1 tablespoon of the olive oil in a small saucepan over medium heat. Add the pumpkin, cover, and cook for 15 minutes, stirring occasionally until the pumpkin is very tender. Remove from the heat, drain off any excess liquid and stir the pumpkin well to form a coarse purée; cool to room temperature.

Put the lamb, onion, allspice and chilli in the bowl of an electric mixer fitted with a paddle attachment and mix on low speed for 5 minutes, or until a little sticky. Add the burghul, puréed pumpkin, sea salt and pepper, and mix for a further 5–6 minutes, or until well combined and elastic. (Alternatively, you can mix the köfte in a large bowl and knead using your hands for 10–12 minutes until elastic.)

Pour half of the remaining olive oil into the base of an 2 litre (8 cup) capacity baking dish, then use your hands to spread half of the burghul mixture evenly over the base of the dish. Scatter over the filling. Take small handfuls of the remaining burghul mixture at a time and flatten them, then arrange them alongside each other to create an even layer over the filling. Using a large sharp knife, cut a diamond pattern in the top of the köfte. Press a walnut half into each diamond, then brush the remaining olive oil over the top of the köfte. Bake in the oven for 40 minutes, or until light golden and cooked through. Remove from the oven and cool slightly before serving warm or at room temperature with the lemon wedges and the roast tomatoes passed separately. **SERVES 8**

350 g (12 oz/2 cups) fine burghul (bulgur)

100 ml (3½ fl oz) extra virgin olive oil

600 g (1 lb 5 oz) jap pumpkin (winter squash), peeled, seeded and chopped

750 g (1 lb 10 oz) minced (ground) lamb

1 onion, finely chopped

½ teaspoon ground allspice

1 teaspoon dried chilli flakes

1 teaspoon sea salt

1 teaspoon freshly ground black pepper

16 walnut halves

lemon wedges, to serve

FILLING

2 tablespoons extra virgin olive oil

300 g (10½ oz) minced (ground) lamb

1 onion, finely chopped

2 garlic cloves, crushed

1 tablespoon tomato paste (concentrated purée)

½ teaspoon ground allspice

½ teaspoon ground cinnamon

1 teaspoon dried chilli flakes

50 g (1¾ oz/½ cup) walnuts, chopped

⅓ cup chopped flat-leaf (Italian) parsley

OREGANO–PAPRIKA ROAST TOMATOES

12 small tomatoes, halved lengthways

1½ teaspoons caster (superfine) sugar

1½ teaspoons sweet paprika

½ teaspoon dried chilli flakes

1 tablespoon oregano leaves

2½ tablespoons olive oil

2½ tablespoons red wine vinegar

TOMATO, RAISIN AND WHEAT PILAF

INGREDIENTS

265 g (9½ oz/1½ cups) coarse burghul
    (bulgur)
80 ml (2½ fl oz/⅓ cup) olive oil
2 onions, finely chopped
2 garlic cloves, crushed
1½ tablespoons tomato paste
    (concentrated purée)
2½ teaspoons ground cumin
30 g (1 oz/¼ cup) chopped sundried tomatoes
40 g (1½ oz/⅓ cup) white raisins (see note)
560 ml (19¼ fl oz/2¼ cups) chicken stock
2 x 1 kg (2 lb 4 oz) lamb rump roasts, trimmed
lemon wedges, to serve
baby spinach salad, to serve

MINTED YOGHURT

500 g (1 lb 2 oz/2 cups) Greek-style yoghurt
1 garlic clove, finely chopped (optional)
3 tablespoons chopped mint

METHOD

To make the minted yoghurt, combine the yoghurt, garlic and mint in a bowl and season with sea salt and freshly ground black pepper. Stir well to combine, then cover and refrigerate until needed.

Rinse the burghul under running water and drain well. Heat 2½ tablespoons of the olive oil in a large saucepan over medium heat. Add the onion and garlic and cook for 5–6 minutes, or until softened. Add the tomato paste, cumin, sundried tomato and white raisins and cook, stirring often, for 3–4 minutes, then add the burghul. Stir to combine, then add the stock and bring to a simmer. Cover, reduce the heat to very low and cook for 15–20 minutes, or until most of the liquid has been absorbed. Remove the pan from the heat and set aside, covered, for 15 minutes, or until the burghul is very tender.

Meanwhile, heat the remaining oil in a heavy-based frying pan over medium heat. Season the lamb rumps with sea salt and freshly ground black pepper and place in the pan. Cover the pan with a lid and cook the roasts for 25 minutes, turning once, until cooked through but still a little pink in the middle. Remove from the heat and rest the meat for 10 minutes before slicing.

To serve, divide the pilaf, lamb, minted yoghurt and lemon wedges among shallow bowls or plates and serve immediately with a spinach salad passed separately. **SERVES 6**

Note: Unlike most raisins, which are sun-dried, white raisins, or muscats, are dried in the oven. They are less sweet than sultanas (golden raisins). You can use regular raisins if white raisins are unavailable.

WILD GREENS, FREEKAH AND PRAWNS WITH SPICY CAPSICUM PUREE

METHOD

To make the capsicum purée, place the capsicums directly over a low flame and cook, turning often, for about 10–15 minutes, or until the skin is blackened all over. (Alternatively, cook the capsicums on a barbecue grill heated to high.) Transfer to a bowl, cover with a tea towel (dish towel) and stand until cool enough to handle. Using your hands, remove the blackened skins and seeds, using a little water to loosen if necessary — do not rinse them in water or you will lose flavour. Tear the capsicum flesh into pieces and set aside.

Heat the olive oil in a saucepan over medium heat. Add the onion and garlic and cook for 6–7 minutes, or until softened. Add the pepper paste, paprika, chilli and cinnamon and cook, stirring, for 2 minutes. Remove from the heat and transfer to a food processor. Add the capsicum and sugar and process to make a coarse purée. Season with sea salt and freshly ground black pepper and refrigerate until needed — bring it back to room temperature before serving.

Put the freekah and 375 ml (13 fl oz/1½ cups) water in a saucepan and bring to a simmer, cover and cook over low heat for 25–30 minutes, or until the water has been absorbed and the freekah is tender. Remove from the heat and set aside.

Remove any tough stems from the cabbage and spinach. Wash all of the greens and drain. Heat half of the olive oil in a very large saucepan, add the garlic and cinnamon stick and cook over medium heat for 2 minutes, or until fragrant. Add the cabbage and 80 ml (2½ fl oz/⅓ cup) water, increase the heat to medium–high, cover and cook for 7–8 minutes, stirring occasionally until tender. Remove to a bowl.

Heat the remaining oil in the same pan and add the spinach, rocket, watercress, dandelion leaves and prawns. Cook, stirring often, for 3–4 minutes, or until the greens have wilted and the prawns are nearly cooked through. Return the cabbage to the pan with the freekah, stir well to combine, then cover and cook for 3 minutes, or until heated through. Season with sea salt and freshly ground black pepper and discard the cinnamon stick. Serve immediately with the capsicum purée passed separately. **SERVES 6**

Note: Freekah is an Arabic food that's eaten in the south of Turkey, where there is a strong Middle Eastern influence. It is a form of wheat, picked while still green, that is then roasted and sun-dried to give it a fantastic smoky flavour.

INGREDIENTS

165 g (5¾ oz/1 cup) freekah (green wheat), rinsed well

1 head Tuscan cabbage

250 g (9 oz) English spinach

100 g (3½ oz) rocket (arugula)

300 g (10½ oz) watercress

100 g (3½ oz) dandelion leaves (optional)

80 ml (2½ fl oz/⅓ cup) extra virgin olive oil

3 garlic cloves, crushed

1 cinnamon stick

1.5 kg (3 lb 5 oz) raw king prawns (shrimp), peeled and deveined

SPICY CAPSICUM PUREE

3 large red capsicums (peppers)

2½ tablespoons olive oil

1 large onion, finely chopped

3 garlic cloves, chopped

1½ tablespoons Turkish pepper paste (see note page 13)

1½ teaspoons sweet paprika

1½ teaspoons dried chilli flakes

½ teaspoon ground cinnamon

1 teaspoon sugar

CHICKEN BILBER DOLMAS

INGREDIENTS

6 green or red banana peppers or 6 x 150 g
    (5½ oz) small red capsicums (peppers)

CHICKEN FILLING

80 ml (2½ fl oz/⅓ cup) extra virgin olive oil

1 onion, finely chopped

1 garlic clove, finely chopped

2 tablespoons pine nuts

100 g (3½ oz/½ cup) long-grain white rice

2 boneless, skinless chicken thighs,
    trimmed and finely chopped

2 teaspoons Turkish pepper paste
    (see note page 13)

2 tablespoons currants

1½ teaspoons caster (superfine) sugar

¼ teaspoon ground cinnamon

¼ teaspoon ground allspice

½ teaspoon sea salt

310 ml (10¾ fl oz/1¼ cups) chicken stock

1½ tablespoons freshly squeezed lemon juice

METHOD

To make the chicken filling, heat half of the olive oil in a saucepan over medium heat. Add the onion, garlic and pine nuts and cook for 5–6 minutes, or until the onion has softened. Add the rice and cook, stirring, for 2 minutes, then add the chicken, pepper paste, currants, sugar, cinnamon, allspice, salt and half of the chicken stock. Bring to a simmer, cover with a tight-fitting lid and cook over low heat for 10 minutes, or until the liquid has been absorbed. Stir in the lemon juice and season with freshly ground black pepper. Remove from the heat and cool slightly.

Cut the tops off the peppers and reserve. Using a teaspoon, remove the seeds and membrane from the peppers and discard. Stuff the peppers with the chicken filling, taking care not to fill them to the top as the rice needs room to expand. Replace the tops of the peppers, then lay them in a deep frying pan so they fit snugly in a single layer. Pour the remaining stock and oil into the pan and cover with a sheet of baking paper. Place a plate over the top to gently weigh them down and cover with a lid. Place over low heat and cook for 45–50 minutes, or until the peppers are tender and the filling is cooked. Serve warm or at room temperature with the cooking liquid spooned over the top.
MAKES 6

BURGHUL PILAF

INGREDIENTS

350 g (12 oz/2 cups) coarse burghul (bulgur)

2½ tablespoons olive oil

1 large onion, finely chopped

1 garlic clove, crushed

1 cinnamon stick

750 ml (26 fl oz/3 cups) chicken stock

METHOD

Wash the burghul under cold running water until the water runs clear, then drain well and set aside.

Heat the olive oil in a large saucepan over medium heat. Add the onion and garlic and cook for 5–6 minutes, stirring often until softened. Add the cinnamon stick and stock, bring to the boil, then reduce the heat to low, cover, and cook for about 12–15 minutes, or until all of the liquid has been absorbed. Season with sea salt and freshly ground black pepper, fluff the grains with a fork. Serve warm or at room temperature. **SERVES 4–6**

RICE PILAF

INGREDIENTS

400 g (14 oz/2 cups) baldo or other
    medium-grain white rice (see note)

50 g (1¾ oz) butter

1 large onion, finely chopped

1 garlic clove, crushed

1 fresh bay leaf

750 ml (26 fl oz/3 cups) chicken stock

METHOD

Wash the rice under cold running water until the water runs clear, then drain well and set aside.

Melt the butter in a large saucepan over medium heat. Add the onion and garlic and cook for 5–6 minutes, stirring often until softened. Add the drained rice and cook for 2–3 minutes, stirring to coat the rice and heat through. Add the bay leaf and stock, bring to the boil, then reduce the heat to low, cover, and cook for 12 minutes, or until all of the liquid has been absorbed. Remove from the heat and stand, covered, for a further 20 minutes, or until the rice is tender. Season with sea salt and freshly ground black pepper, fluff the grains with a fork, and serve warm or at room temperature. **SERVES 4–6**

Note: Baldo rice is an Italian medium-grain rice. This rice variety is also grown in Turkey and is perfect for making pilafs and dolma fillings as it holds its shape well when cooked and is not sticky.

SILVERBEET AND BURGHUL PILAF WITH SPICED ONIONS

Heat 2 tablespoons of the olive oil in a large, heavy-based frying pan over medium heat. Add the onion and cook for 15–18 minutes, or until deep golden. Add the allspice, paprika and chilli, season with sea salt and freshly ground black pepper, and continue cooking for 1–2 minutes, or until fragrant. Remove from the heat and set aside until needed.

Remove the stems and any thick veins from the silverbeet leaves, discarding any tough or damaged outer leaves. Trim 2 cm ($^3/_4$ inch) from the ends of the stems, then finely chop the stems and veins. Rinse and dry the leaves, then finely chop them and set aside. Heat the remaining olive oil in a large saucepan over medium heat. Add the chopped silverbeet stems to the pan, cover, and cook for 10 minutes, stirring often, until softened. Add the barberries, burghul and stock to the pan, stirring well to combine, then bring the mixture to a simmer. Cover the pan and cook over low heat for about 15–20 minutes, or until the burghul is almost tender. Remove from the heat and stand for 5 minutes. Season with sea salt and freshly ground black pepper and fluff with a fork.

Meanwhile, fill a saucepan with about 3 cm (1$^1/_4$ inches) water and bring to the boil. Add the reserved silverbeet leaves, cover with a tight-fitting lid, and cook for 5 minutes, or until tender. Drain in a colander, cool, then use your hands to press down and extract as much liquid as possible. Combine in a bowl with the yoghurt and garlic, season with sea salt and freshly ground black pepper, then cover with plastic wrap and refrigerate until needed.

Serve the pilaf warm or at room temperature with the spiced onions and yoghurt mixture. **SERVES 6**

Note: Barberries are sour little fruits from a shrub, available from Middle Eastern grocery stores. They lend a pretty pink colour and refreshingly tart kick to dishes such as this pilaf.

80 ml (2$^1/_2$ fl oz/$^1/_3$ cup) extra virgin olive oil

3 large onions, thinly sliced

1 teaspoon ground allspice

1 teaspoon sweet paprika

1 teaspoon dried chilli flakes (optional)

800 g (1 lb 12 oz) silverbeet (Swiss chard)

50 g (1$^3/_4$ oz/$^1/_3$ cup) dried barberries (see note)

265 g (9$^1/_2$ oz/1$^1/_2$ cups) coarse burghul (bulgur)

500 ml (17 fl oz/2 cups) chicken stock

375 g (13 oz/1$^1/_2$ cups) Greek-style yoghurt

2 garlic cloves, crushed

MAKING PEKMEZ AND PESTIL IN THE COUNTRYSIDE

Pekmez is a defining ingredient of Turkish cooking — it's the molasses-like syrup that results from the boiling down of fruit must. It's thick, gooey and dark and, as a precursor of sugar, is an ancient food. A variety of fruits are used for pekmez, such as pears, mulberries, plums, figs and even carob. But arguably the most common type is made from grapes. Pekmez is used to flavour fruit compotes and rustic desserts, such as flour halva and is eaten, with tahini, for breakfast with bread. I learn it is also used medicinally, in much the same way balsamic vinegar is in Italy; a spoonful every morning is said to be good for whatever might ail you.

I'm in Diyarbakir in autumn when my friend Mehmet invites me to his parents' village about thirty kilometres away to see pekmez being made. We hop on a bus that will drop us nearby and end up walking the last few kilometres through the hot sun on dusty roads.

We soon forget how uncomfortable we are when we reach fields thick with wild thyme. Its sweet, piney fragrance is released with every footfall. We're quite elevated here and enjoy sweeping vistas of agricultural land. Our path turns through grape vines as we approach Mehmet's mum, dad, and various other relatives who are hard at work making pestil, a dried, leathery fruit paste. For this, grapes have been boiled down to a thick purée, strained and then spread thinly and evenly over sheets of cloth. These are left to dry in the sun until the fruit has a pliable, leathery texture. Then it is cut into manageable pieces and put aside for use as a sustaining snack for the year ahead. It takes five people to make it; one person holds each of the corners of the cloth while the fifth person spreads on the paste.

We then watch as the men take turns to stir the grape pulp that is slowly reducing down into pekmez. It cooks in an enormous cauldron set over a wood fire and while the process is simple, the work is hot, hard and goes on for hours. The family spends three days labouring here to get the pekmez and pestil made, using the same processes and equipment employed for centuries. It's a scene played out through much of rural Turkey year round and reminds me, along with other acts of preserving the harvest that I've seen (drying fruits and vegetables and making sun-dried pastes, for example), that in some parts of the country at least, there is still a reliance on what the seasons offer for food.

Kisir is the tabouleh of Turkey, although it contains a good deal less parsley and has a lovely reddish hue from the vegetable paste, tomato and spices. To me it begs for the addition of rare-grilled tuna or salmon. In Turkey it is usually served as a meze or side dish with grilled lamb, beef or fish.

KISIR

INGREDIENTS

750 g (1 lb 10 oz) tuna steaks

olive oil, for brushing

350 g (12 oz/2 cups) fine burghul (bulgur)

80 ml (2½ fl oz/⅓ cup) extra virgin olive oil, plus extra, for cooking

1 onion, finely chopped

2 garlic cloves, crushed

1 tablespoon tomato paste (concentrated purée)

1 tablespoon Turkish pepper paste (see note page 13)

1½ teaspoons ground cumin

2 teaspoons dried chilli flakes

3 firm, ripe tomatoes, finely chopped

2 Lebanese (short) cucumbers, finely chopped

2 teaspoons dried mint

1½ tablespoons pomegranate molasses (see note page 25)

2½ tablespoons freshly squeezed lemon juice, or to taste

⅓ cup chopped flat-leaf (Italian) parsley

⅓ cup chopped mint leaves

lemon wedges, to serve

METHOD

Preheat a chargrill pan or barbecue grill to medium–high. Brush the tuna steaks with the olive oil to coat and cook for about 2 minutes on each side, or until cooked through but still a little pink in the middle. Season with sea salt and freshly ground black pepper, then remove from the heat and allow to cool to room temperature. Break into large pieces and set aside.

Meanwhile, put the burghul in a large bowl and pour over 500 ml (17 fl oz/ 2 cups) boiling water. Cover and leave to soak for 10–15 minutes, or until the water has been absorbed.

Meanwhile, heat the extra virgin olive oil in a small frying pan over medium heat, add the onion and garlic and cook for 5–7 minutes, or until softened. Stir in the tomato paste and pepper paste, cumin and chilli, and cook for 2–3 minutes, or until fragrant. Remove from the heat, cool to room temperature, then stir the mixture into the burghul. Add the tomato, cucumber, mint, pomegranate molasses and lemon juice, tossing to mix well. Add the tuna and toss gently to combine; season, to taste, scatter with the parsley and mint leaves and serve immediately with lemon wedges on the side. **SERVES 6**

Mussels stuffed with rice are a popular street food in Istanbul. The flavours in this pilaf mirror those of the stuffed version, but the pilaf is much easier to make. You can eat this meal hot, but it actually tastes better at room temperature.

MUSSEL, DILL AND CURRANT PILAF

METHOD

Put the rice and salt in a bowl and pour over enough boiling water to cover. Set aside for 30 minutes to soak, then drain well.

Meanwhile, bring 500 ml (17 fl oz/2 cups) water to the boil in a large saucepan. Add the mussels, cover, and cook for 2–3 minutes, shaking the pan occasionally, until the mussels have just opened; discard any that do not open. Remove the mussels to a bowl, then strain and reserve the cooking liquid — add enough water to make 500 ml (17 fl oz/2 cups). When cool enough to handle, remove the mussel meat from the shells, cover and refrigerate until required.

Heat the oil in a large saucepan over medium heat. Add the onion and garlic and cook for 5–7 minutes, or until softened. Add the pine nuts, currants, allspice and rice and cook for 2–3 minutes, stirring well to combine, until the rice is heated through. Add the reserved mussel liquid and bring to the boil, stirring well. Reduce the heat to a simmer, cover, and cook for 15 minutes, or until the liquid has been absorbed. Remove from the heat and stand for 5 minutes. Add the mussels, stir well to combine, then cover and stand for another 5 minutes before serving. **SERVES 6**

INGREDIENTS

280 g (10 oz/1½ cups) baldo rice or other medium-grain white rice (see note page 140)

2 teaspoons salt

1.7 kg (3 lb 12 oz) black mussels, beards removed and shells scrubbed

60 ml (2 fl oz/¼ cup) extra virgin olive oil

1 large onion, finely chopped

2 garlic cloves, finely chopped

50 g (1¾ oz/⅓ cup) pine nuts, toasted

50 g (1¾ oz/⅓ cup) currants

¾ teaspoon ground allspice

⅓ cup chopped dill

L.AYVALIK
Nº 683

FISH AND SEAFOOD

At many Turkish markets a dazzling array of fish, either bright-eyed and on ice, or still alive and thrashing in a tub of water, can be found. This bounty speaks of the kilometres of coastline strung around the Turkish borders where the Black, Marmara, Aegean and Mediterranean seas lap. Red mullet, trout, bonito, mackerel, sea bass, sea perch, tuna, swordfish and sardines are popular, as are squid and mussels. These are subject to the simplest of treatments — grilling or baking usually — and are served with unfussy accompaniments, leaving the fish tasting of the sea, river or stream from which it was plucked.

MACKEREL WITH ONIONS, APPLE CIDER VINEGAR, CUMIN AND CHICKPEAS

METHOD

Preheat the oven to 200°C (400°F/Gas 6). Cook the chickpeas in boiling salted water for 45 minutes, or until tender. Drain well.

Heat the olive oil in a large saucepan over medium heat. Add the onion, garlic and cumin seeds and cook for 6–7 minutes, or until softened. Add the stock, vinegar and chickpeas, then season with sea salt and freshly ground black pepper. Bring to a simmer, then reduce the heat to low and keep warm.

Arrange the mackerel in a single layer in a large baking dish and season with sea salt and freshly ground black pepper. Pour over the hot chickpea mixture, scatter over the chilli, then cover the dish tightly with foil. Bake in the oven for about 7–8 minutes, or until the fish is just cooked through. Serve with boiled potatoes and a green salad passed separately. **SERVES 6**

INGREDIENTS

220 g (7³/₄ oz/1 cup) dried chickpeas, soaked overnight and drained

60 ml (2 fl oz/¹/₄ cup) extra virgin olive oil

3 large red onions, thinly sliced

2 garlic cloves, finely chopped

1 teaspoon cumin seeds, lightly crushed

500 ml (17 fl oz/2 cups) fish or chicken stock

60 ml (2 fl oz/¹/₄ cup) apple cider vinegar

6 x 175 g (6 oz) mackerel cutlets

1 teaspoon dried chilli flakes, or to taste

SEMOLINA-CRUSTED WHITING WITH TOMATO, POMEGRANATE AND SUMAC RELISH

INGREDIENTS

75 g (2³/₄ oz/¹/₂ cup) polenta

12 whole red spot whiting or other small
firm white fish, cleaned

80 ml (2¹/₂ fl oz/¹/₃ cup) olive oil

lemon wedges, to serve

TOMATO, POMEGRANATE AND SUMAC RELISH

5 roma (plum) tomatoes, seeded and
finely chopped

1 small red onion, finely chopped

2¹/₂ teaspoons caster (superfine) sugar

1 tablespoon pomegranate molasses (see note
page 25)

1 tablespoon freshly squeezed lemon juice

1 teaspoon dried chilli flakes

1¹/₂ teaspoons sumac

60 ml (2 fl oz/¹/₄ cup) extra virgin olive oil

1 cup flat-leaf (Italian) parsley leaves,
chopped

1 cup coriander (cilantro) leaves, chopped

METHOD

To make the tomato, pomegranate and sumac relish, combine all of the ingredients in a bowl, season with sea salt and freshly ground black pepper, then cover and stand at room temperature for 1 hour for the flavours to develop.

Put the polenta on a large flat plate and press the fish into the polenta, turning to coat evenly on both sides.

Heat the oil in a large non-stick frying pan over medium–low heat. Add the fish to the pan, laying them in a single layer and alternating heads to tails so they fit snugly. Cook for 6 minutes. Remove from the heat and place a flat tray over the top of the pan. Invert the pan carefully, so that the fish land on the tray, then carefully slide the fish back into the frying pan, taking care not to break the polenta coating. Cook for another 3–4 minutes, or until cooked through. Slide the fish onto serving plates and serve immediately with lemon wedges and the tomato, pomegranate and sumac relish on the side. **SERVES 4**

Where would Turkey be without raki? This non-sweet, anise-flavoured rocket fuel is the social lubricant of choice and is most enjoyed as an accompaniment to meze. It's unlikely that many Turks would cook with it, although it works extremely well here splashed over baking fish.

BAKED FISH WITH DILL BUTTER AND RAKI, ROAST TOMATOES AND PINE NUTS

METHOD

Preheat the oven to 200°C (400°F/Gas 6). Combine the butter, dill, garlic, lemon zest and pepper in a bowl, and stir well to combine.

Using a large, sharp knife, cut four diagonal slits into the flesh of the fish on both sides. Place the butter mixture inside the slits. Place the fish side by side in a large roasting tin and season with sea salt. Scatter over the tomatoes and pine nuts, if using, then drizzle over the raki. Bake in the oven for 20–25 minutes, or until the fish is just cooked through in the middle. Serve immediately with a green salad and flat bread passed separately. **SERVES 4**

INGREDIENTS

80 g (2³/₄ oz) butter, softened

¹/₂ cup chopped dill

2 garlic cloves, crushed

1¹/₂ teaspoons finely grated lemon zest

1 teaspoon freshly ground black pepper

4 x 350 g (12 oz) whole bream, snapper, barramundi or other firm white fish, cleaned

400 g (14 oz) small yellow truss tomatoes

2¹/₂ tablespoons pine nuts, lightly toasted (optional)

100 ml (3¹/₂ fl oz) raki or ouzo

green salad, to serve

flat bread (see page 63), to serve

A FERRY RIDE TO CIYA

I can't remember how I first discovered Ciya, the now famous restaurant in Kadikoy, on the Asian side of Istanbul. Its existence is hardly a secret — Chef Musa Dagdeverin is something of a culinary legend, not only in Turkey but overseas as well. All I know is, Ciya is my refuelling stop of choice in Istanbul. Partly this is to do with the ferry trip required to get there. Taking a commuter ferry is one of the defining experiences of a trip to Istanbul. Complete with precarious gangplanks, wooden seats and decking, and roving hawkers dispensing glasses of hot tea, ferries are a constant presence on the Bosporus. They crisscross the water between some twenty-seven stops, ducking between fishing boats and oil tankers with a token entourage of gliding gulls constantly in tow. From a ferry deck the vistas of the city are spectacular.

While it is not a pretty place, Kadikoy bristles with energy and for a slice of 'everyday' Istanbul it can't be topped. There are wide, busy streets flanked by banks and dull chain stores masking scruffy back lanes full of secondhand bookshops and antique stores. There are old mosques, a sprinkling of historic churches and even one of Istanbul's oldest synagogues, the Hemdat Israel. Kadikoy has a fabulous food market too, strung out along Bahariye Caddesi. It's a lively place to wander around and try something new, such as the so-called 'mad' honey from the Black Sea, olives from Bodrum, or new-season hazelnuts from Giresun.

Ciya is not one, but several neighbouring restaurants. My favourite of these is Ciya Sofrasi, where the menu, which changes daily, is served in the casual style of a lokanta. A lokanta is a genre of restaurant common throughout Turkey where simple food is served from bain-maries, ready-to-go. For some twenty-five years, Dagdeverin has been researching and documenting traditional dishes, including many in danger of dying out completely. Thus a meal at Ciya is something of an exercise in food anthropology — you dine here on fare you'd be hard pressed to find anywhere else. Over a thousand dishes are rotated through the kitchen each year so depending on the season there might be a chestnut, lamb, apple, onion and chickpea soup, lamb chops with quinces, loquats baked with lamb, stuffed spleen, or milk thistle braised with lamb and lemon. The sweet candied fruits and vegetables are legendary and the secret to their jewel-like transparency is a thorough soaking in limewater before cooking. I leave, as I always do, with a feeling of deep contentment and the promise to return.

SALT-BAKED FISH WITH BEETROOT SALAD AND PISTACHIO AND TAHINI SAUCE

INGREDIENTS

4 kg (9 lb) coarse sea salt

2 egg whites, lightly beaten

3 kg (6 lb 12 oz) whole snapper, cleaned
with scales left on

BEETROOT SALAD

1 kg (2 lb 4 oz) beetroot (beets), trimmed and
scrubbed clean

300 ml (10½ fl oz) olive oil

50 g (1¾ oz/⅓ cup) currants

2 garlic cloves, crushed

1 egg yolk

1 tablespoon dijon mustard

60 ml (2 fl oz/¼ cup) red wine vinegar

60 g (2¼ oz/½ cup) semi-dried black olives

1 head radicchio, trimmed, tough outer
leaves discarded, leaves torn

3 tablespoons coriander
(cilantro), leaves chopped

PISTACHIO AND TAHINI SAUCE

1 thick slice day-old rustic bread,
crusts removed

210 g (7½ oz/1½ cups) pistachios

2 garlic cloves, chopped

2 tablespoons tahini

60 ml (2 fl oz/¼ cup) freshly squeezed
lemon juice

2½ tablespoons olive oil

METHOD

Preheat the oven to 180°C (350°F/Gas 4).

To make the beetroot salad, place the beetroot in a small baking dish, add 2½ tablespoons of the olive oil and toss to coat. Roast for 1½ hours or until tender — insert a skewer into the centres to check if they are done. When cool enough to handle remove the skins and cut into 1.5 cm (⅝ inch) thick wedges. Put the currants in a small bowl and pour over just enough boiling water to cover. Leave to soak for 10 minutes, then drain well. Combine the garlic, egg yolk, mustard and vinegar in a bowl and whisk well to combine. Whisking constantly, add the remaining olive oil in a slow, steady stream until the mixture is thickened and emulsified. Stir in the currants and season with sea salt and freshly ground black pepper. Combine the beetroot in a bowl with the olives and radicchio, season with sea salt and freshly ground black pepper, tossing well to combine. Drizzle over the dressing and scatter over the coriander. Cover with plastic wrap and refrigerate until ready to serve.

To make the pistachio and tahini sauce, soak the bread in a bowl of water, then use your hands to squeeze as much water out as possible. Place in a food processor with the pistachios and garlic and process until the nuts are very finely chopped. Add the remaining ingredients and process well to combine. Using the pulse button, add 125 ml (4 fl oz/½ cup) water or just enough to create a smooth pouring consistency; season with sea salt and freshly ground black pepper. Set aside until ready to serve.

When you are ready to cook the fish, increase the oven temperature to 220°C (425°F/Gas 7). Combine the sea salt and egg whites in a large bowl and stir well to combine. Spread one-third of the salt mixture in the base of a baking dish large enough to hold the fish, then place the fish on top. Press the remaining salt mixture over the top of the fish, packing to seal and enclose (the tail may protrude slightly). Bake the fish in the oven for about 55 minutes, or until the salt has formed a very hard crust. Using a meat mallet, crack open the crust, using your hands to pull off the salt. Peel off and discard the skin, then serve the fish immediately with the pistachio and tahini sauce and beetroot salad passed separately. **SERVES 6–8**

BAKED SQUID STUFFED WITH ORANGE, HERBS AND CURRANTS

INGREDIENTS

6 x 200 g (7 oz) squid, cleaned — tubes, wings
    and tentacles reserved separately

125 ml (4 fl oz/$\frac{1}{2}$ cup) extra virgin olive oil

1 onion, finely chopped

3 garlic cloves

50 g (1$\frac{3}{4}$ oz/$\frac{1}{3}$ cup) currants

50 g (1$\frac{3}{4}$ oz/$\frac{1}{3}$ cup) pistachios, chopped

100 g (3$\frac{1}{2}$ oz/1$\frac{1}{4}$ cups) fresh breadcrumbs

125 g (4$\frac{1}{2}$ oz) feta cheese, crumbled

1$\frac{1}{2}$ teaspoons finely grated orange zest

1 cup flat-leaf (Italian) parsley leaves,
    chopped, plus extra, to serve

2 tablespoons chopped oregano leaves

$\frac{1}{2}$ teaspoon dried chilli flakes, or to taste

1 egg, lightly beaten

700 g (1 lb 9 oz) kipfler potatoes, peeled

5 tomatoes, quartered

2 red capsicums (peppers), seeded,
    membrane removed and cut into 3 cm
    (1$\frac{1}{4}$ inch) pieces

90 g (3$\frac{1}{4}$ oz/$\frac{1}{2}$ cup) pitted green olives

1 tablespoon tomato paste
    (concentrated purée)

310 ml (10$\frac{3}{4}$ fl oz/1$\frac{1}{4}$ cups) freshly squeezed
    orange juice

METHOD

Finely chop the squid wings. Heat 2 tablespoons of the olive oil in a saucepan over medium–low heat. Add the onion, garlic, currants and pistachios and cook for 5–7 minutes, or until the onion has softened. Remove from the heat and cool slightly, then add to a bowl with the chopped squid, breadcrumbs, feta, orange zest, parsley, oregano and chilli, stirring to mix well. Season with sea salt and freshly ground black pepper, then add the egg and stir well to combine.

Preheat the oven to 160°C (315°F/Gas 2–3). Carefully spoon the filling into the squid tubes, taking care not to fill them too much or they might burst during cooking.

Combine the potatoes, tomato, capsicum, olives, tomato paste, remaining olive oil and orange juice in a large baking dish and toss to coat. Season to taste, then arrange the stuffed squid tubes and reserved tentacles in a single layer in the base of the dish. Cover the dish tightly with foil and bake for 1 hour 20 minutes, or until the vegetables and squid are very tender. Serve with the extra parsley sprinkled on top and a green salad passed separately. **SERVES 6**

FISH PILAKI WITH CELERIAC, PINK GRAPEFRUIT JUICE, TOMATO AND OREGANO

Put the saffron in a bowl with 2 tablespoons hot water and leave to stand for 1 hour or until deep orange. Peel the celeriac and cut it into 8 mm (³⁄₈ inch) pieces, then place in a bowl of acidulated water (see note page 107).

Heat 80 ml (2 fl oz/¹⁄₃ cup) of the olive oil in a saucepan over medium–low heat. Add the onion and cook for 4–5 minutes, or until softened. Add the drained celeriac and stir to coat, then add the saffron mixture, grapefruit juice, lemon juice and bay leaf and bring to a gentle simmer for 7–8 minutes, or until the vegetables are tender. Season with sea salt and freshly ground black pepper, then stir in the tomato and olives. Cover and keep warm.

Heat the remaining oil in a large frying pan over medium heat. Dust the fish in the flour, shaking off any excess, then cook for 6–7 minutes, turning once, or until just cooked. Season the fish fillets, then transfer to a large serving platter and spoon the celeriac over the top. Sprinkle with the oregano and serve immediately or at room temperature with a green salad passed separately. **SERVES 4**

INGREDIENTS

1 large pinch saffron threads

700 g (1 lb 9 oz) celeriac, trimmed

60 ml (2 fl oz/¹⁄₄ cup) freshly squeezed lemon juice

2 onions, finely chopped

125 ml (4 fl oz/¹⁄₂ cup) extra virgin olive oil

500 ml (17 fl oz/2 cups) freshly squeezed pink grapefruit juice

1 fresh bay leaf, bruised

3 vine-ripened tomatoes, trimmed and finely chopped

60 g (2¹⁄₄ oz/¹⁄₂ cup) Ligurian or other small olives

6 x 175 g (6 oz) snapper fillets, skin on

plain (all-purpose) flour, for dusting

2 tablespoons chopped oregano

SPICE-FRIED CALAMARI AND GARLIC SAUCE

INGREDIENTS

100 g (3½ oz) cornflour (cornstarch)

125 g (4½ oz) plain (all-purpose) flour,
    plus extra, for dusting

½ teaspoon baking powder

1 teaspoon salt

300 ml (10½ fl oz) beer

2½ teaspoons cumin seeds

2½ teaspoons dried chilli flakes

2½ teaspoons paprika

1 teaspoon freshly ground black pepper

vegetable oil, for deep-frying

1 kg (2 lb 4 oz) squid, cleaned, tubes cut into
    12 x 6 cm (4½ x 2½ inch) pieces, tentacles
    left whole

½ cup basil leaves

½ cup flat-leaf (Italian) parsley leaves

lemon wedges, to serve

GARLIC SAUCE

2 thick slices day-old rustic bread,
    crusts removed

5 garlic cloves, chopped

185 ml (6 fl oz/¾ cup) extra virgin olive oil

60 ml (2 fl oz/¼ cup) freshly squeezed lemon
    juice, or to taste

2½ tablespoons chopped flat-leaf
    (Italian) parsley

METHOD

To make the garlic sauce, soak the bread in a bowl of water, then use your hands to squeeze as much water out as possible. Place in a food processor with the remaining ingredients and process to make a chunky paste; season with sea salt. Set aside until needed.

Sift the cornflour, flour, baking powder and salt into a bowl and make a well in the centre. Add the beer and whisk constantly to make a smooth batter. Stir in the cumin seeds, chilli, paprika and pepper.

Fill a deep-fryer or large heavy-based saucepan two-thirds full of oil and heat to 180°C (350°F), or until a cube of bread dropped into the oil turns golden in 15 seconds. Make sure the basil and parsley leaves are well dried before you cook them. Deep-fry the herb leaves, in batches, for 2–3 minutes each, or until crisp. Remove carefully from the oil to a plate lined with paper towels to drain.

Working quickly, dust the squid in the spiced flour, shaking off the excess. Working in batches, dip the squid into the batter and drain off the excess. Deep-fry the squid for 2 minutes, or until the batter is puffed and golden, then remove using a slotted spoon and drain the excess oil on paper towels. Repeat until all of the squid is cooked.

Serve immediately with the garlic sauce and lemon wedges on the side, and the crisp herbs scattered over. **SERVES 6**

FISH KÖFTE WITH PICKLED GREEN BEANS AND LEMON CREME FRAICHE

METHOD

To make the pickled green beans, put the vinegar, garlic, allspice, peppercorns, chillies, bay leaf, salt and 750 ml (26 fl oz/3 cups) water in a saucepan. Bring slowly to a simmer, stirring to dissolve the salt, then remove from the heat and cool to room temperature. Meanwhile, blanch the beans in a saucepan of boiling water for 2 minutes. Drain well, then plunge into a large bowl of iced water to cool. Drain. Place the beans in a large sterilised airtight jar and pour over the vinegar mixture, pushing the beans down to cover. Seal the jar, then refrigerate for at least 2 days before using. The beans can be stored in the brine in the refrigerator for up to 1 month.

To make the lemon crème fraîche, combine the crème fraîche and lemon zest in a small bowl, season with sea salt and freshly ground black pepper, then cover with plastic wrap and refrigerate until needed.

To make the köfte, put the currants in a small bowl and pour over enough boiling water to just cover. Leave to soak for 10 minutes, then drain well and pat dry on paper towels. Place the burghul in a bowl and add enough cold water to just cover, then leave to soak for 10 minutes. Drain well in a fine sieve, pressing with your hands to remove as much liquid as possible.

Finely chop 200 g (7 oz) of the fish into 5 mm ($^1/_4$ inch) pieces and set aside. Coarsely chop the remaining fish and combine with the currants and drained burghul in a food processor. Add the tomato paste, pepper paste, allspice, dill, parsley and chilli and process until smooth and well combined. Season with sea salt and freshly ground black pepper. Remove to a bowl and gently mix in the reserved fish. Cover with plastic wrap and refrigerate for 1 hour to firm slightly.

Take 1 heaped tablespoon of the mixture at a time and form into a slightly tapered torpedo shape. Repeat with the remaining mixture, then dust the köfte lightly with flour, shaking off any excess.

Heat the olive oil in a large heavy-based frying pan over medium heat. Cook the köfte, in batches, for 6–7 minutes, turning often and adding more oil as necessary, or until golden and cooked through. Remove with a slotted spoon then drain on paper towels. Serve the fish köfte with the pickled green beans and lemon crème fraîche. **SERVES 6**

INGREDIENTS

2$^1/_2$ tablespoons currants
60 g (2$^1/_4$ oz/$^1/_3$ cup) fine burghul (bulgur)
700 g (1 lb 9 oz) skinless, boneless
    kingfish fillets
2 teaspoons tomato paste
    (concentrated purée)
2 teaspoons Turkish pepper paste
    (see note page 13)
$^3/_4$ teaspoon ground allspice
2$^1/_2$ tablespoons chopped dill
1 cup flat-leaf (Italian) parsley leaves,
    chopped
1 large pinch dried chilli flakes
plain (all-purpose) flour, for dusting
125 ml (4 fl oz/$^1/_2$ cup) olive oil

PICKLED GREEN BEANS

250 ml (9 fl oz/1 cup) white vinegar
3 garlic cloves, bruised
1 teaspoon whole allspice berries
1 teaspoon black peppercorns
4 whole dried chillies
2 fresh bay leaves, bruised
2 tablespoons sea salt
500 g (1 lb 2 oz) green beans trimmed

LEMON CREME FRAICHE

250 g (9 oz/1 cup) crème fraîche
2$^1/_2$ teaspoons finely grated lemon zest

LAKE VAN AND THE RARE AND DELICIOUS PEARL MULLET

In Turkey, I've had amazing experiences meeting with perfect strangers. Nowhere more than in Van, in the south of the Armenian Highlands. The big attraction in this part of the world is Lake Van, the largest lake in Turkey, which is a whopping 119 kilometres across at its widest point. Within the lake are four islands, and when I'm in Van, I'm invited over to visit the second largest of these, Akdamar Island.

My new friend takes me on a ferry ride to Akdamar to see the thousand-year-old Cathedral of the Holy Cross, an architecturally important pink sandstone church erected by the Armenian catholics. The exterior is liberally decorated with bas-relief carvings depicting biblical scenes. From the island we look back over the sparkling lake to the vast, open expanse of land on the other side where farmers are fashioning dried grass into huge round bales of hay. Behind this farmland lies a string of snow-capped mountain peaks. It's a place of dramatic and breathtaking beauty and it's fitting that we finish our day-trip off by gorging on the local delicacy, inci kefali or pearl mullet.

This fish is one of the few that can survive the highly alkaline conditions of Lake Van whose waters have a pH of 9.8. These critters have been an important food here for a long time — in the past they were eaten un-gutted, or simply salted and dried during the long arctic winters. When I visit, the season for the fish spawning is nearly finished, so we're lucky we can still order some from the roadside restaurant near the Akdamar ferry port. The mullet are cooked very simply — either fried, grilled or baked. In season, the mullet are a popular worker's meal — the fish are taken on large rectangular pans to the local baker who bakes them in his oven for lunch. Today, ours are deep-fried to heavenly crunchy crispness. The fish are picky to eat, their flesh riddled with fine, sharp bones, but they taste sweet, with a not-unpleasant, muddy note.

Afterwards, on the mainland, we stop at the resort town of Edremit to take in the views from the hill above town. It's cool, up high, but the views over the blue, shimmering lake are magical. Around us, local families stoke up fires for early evening barbecues. Women sit with boards on their knees, chopping tomatoes and onions for salad and peeling charred, fat capsicums. They invite us to share their food later but sadly, we're too stuffed full of fish.

A güveç is an uncomplicated all-in-one baked dish commonly cooked in Turkey. The word güveç simply means 'earthernware pot' and the traditional shallow clay vessel is sealed and cooked in a tandoor oven, which imparts a magical flavour. This then is the cheat's version, but the flavours mingle beautifully nonetheless.

PRAWN GÜVEÇ

METHOD

Preheat the oven to 180°C (350°F/Gas 4). Heat the olive oil in a large ovenproof frying pan over medium heat. Add the onion and cook for 4–5 minutes, or until beginning to soften. Add the capsicum and garlic and cook, stirring, for 5 minutes. Scatter over the sugar and drizzle with the vinegar, then transfer to the oven and cook for 15 minutes, or until the vegetables are starting to brown slightly. Add the cherry tomatoes, oregano, paprika, allspice, prawns and feta, season with sea salt and freshly ground black pepper, and gently toss to combine. Return to the oven and bake for a further 10–15 minutes, or until the prawns are just cooked through. Sprinkle with the parsley and serve immediately with the crusty bread and green salad passed separately. **SERVES 6**

INGREDIENTS

80 ml (2½ fl oz /⅓ cup) extra virgin olive oil

2 large red onions, cut into 1.5 cm (⅝ inch) pieces

2 red capsicums (peppers), membrane removed, seeded and cut into 2 cm (¾ inch) pieces

1 large yellow capsicum (pepper), seeded, membrane removed and cut into 2 cm (¾ inch) pieces

4 garlic cloves, chopped

1 tablespoon caster (superfine) sugar

1½ tablespoons red wine vinegar

500 g (1 lb 2 oz) cherry tomatoes, halved

2½ tablespoons chopped oregano

1 teaspoon paprika

½ teaspoon ground allspice

2 kg (4 lb 8 oz) raw king prawns (shrimp), peeled and deveined

175 g (6 oz) feta cheese, coarsely crumbled

3 tablespoons chopped flat-leaf (Italian) parsley

rustic bread slices, to serve

green salad, to serve

GRILLED BLUE-EYE WITH SAFFRON FENNEL AND ALMOND TARATOR

INGREDIENTS

6 x 185 g (6½ oz) boneless blue-eye fillets,
    skin on
2 tablespoons olive oil
boiled potatoes, to serve

ALMOND TARATOR

1 thick slice day-old rustic bread,
    crusts trimmed
175 g (6 oz) blanched almonds, chopped
2 garlic cloves, crushed
½ teaspoon ground cinnamon
60 ml (2 fl oz/¼ cup) white wine vinegar
80 ml (2½ fl oz/⅓ cup) extra virgin olive oil

SAFFRON FENNEL

½ teaspoon saffron threads
80 ml (2½ fl oz/⅓ cup) olive oil
2 fennel bulbs, trimmed, halved lengthways
    and cut into wedges
1½ tablespoons freshly squeezed lemon juice
2½ teaspoons caster (superfine) sugar

METHOD

To make the almond tarator, soak the bread in a bowl of water, then use your hands to squeeze as much excess water out as possible. Combine the bread with the remaining ingredients in a food processor and process to make a coarse paste. Season with sea salt and freshly ground black pepper — the tarator should have a thick, creamy consistency, you may need to thin with a little warm water to achieve the right consistency. Set aside.

To make the saffron fennel, soak the saffron threads in 2 tablespoons hot water for 40 minutes. Preheat the oven to 180°C (350°F/Gas 4). Heat the olive oil in a large heavy-based frying pan over medium heat. Add the fennel, in batches, and cook for 3 minutes on each side, or until light golden. Transfer with any pan juices to a large baking dish. Sprinkle over the lemon juice, sugar and the saffron mixture and season with sea salt and freshly ground black pepper. Cover the dish tightly with foil and bake for 1–1½ hours, or until the fennel is very tender. Keep warm until ready to serve.

Heat a chargrill or barbecue grill to medium–high. Brush the fish with olive oil and season to taste, then cook for about 3 minutes on each side, or until just cooked through. Serve with the boiled potatoes and saffron fennel, with the almond tarator spooned over the top. **SERVES 6**

OCTOPUS STEW WITH WINE, SPICES AND CAPERBERRIES

METHOD

Heat the olive oil in a large saucepan over medium heat. Add the onion, carrot and garlic and cook for 5–7 minutes, or until the onion has softened. Add the octopus, pepper paste, tomato paste, paprika, allspice, chilli and cinnamon, and cook for 2 minutes, or until fragrant. Add the wine and vinegar and bring the mixture to a simmer, then reduce the heat to low, cover, and cook for 1 hour. Remove the lid and continue simmering uncovered for another 30 minutes, or until the octopus is tender. Remove from the heat, stir through the caperberries and parsley and serve immediately. **SERVES 6**

INGREDIENTS

$2^{1}/_{2}$ tablespoons olive oil

2 onions, chopped

2 carrots, cut into 5 mm ($^{1}/_{4}$ inch) thick rings

3 garlic cloves, crushed

1.25 kg (2 lb 12 oz) baby octopus, cleaned

$2^{1}/_{2}$ tablespoons Turkish pepper paste (see note page 13)

$1^{1}/_{2}$ tablespoons tomato paste (concentrated purée)

2 teaspoons paprika

$1^{1}/_{2}$ teaspoons ground allspice

1 teaspoon dried chilli flakes

1 cinnamon stick

300 ml ($10^{1}/_{2}$ fl oz) red wine

$1^{1}/_{2}$ tablespoons red wine vinegar

90 g ($3^{1}/_{4}$ oz/$^{3}/_{4}$ cup) caperberries

$^{1}/_{2}$ cup chopped flat-leaf (Italian) parsley

SARDINES WITH THYME–PAPRIKA CRUMBS AND POTATO-GARLIC PUREE

METHOD

To make the potato–garlic purée, cook the potatoes in a saucepan of boiling water for 15–20 minutes, or until tender. Push the potatoes through a potato ricer into a bowl or use a potato masher to mash well. Add the remaining ingredients and stir well to combine; season with sea salt and freshly ground black pepper. Set aside and keep warm.

Preheat the oven to 180°C (350°F/Gas 4). Heat 80 ml (2½ fl oz/⅓ cup) of the olive oil in a heavy-based ovenproof frying pan over medium heat. Add the breadcrumbs, onion, garlic, paprika and chilli flakes and stir well to combine. Bake in the oven for 20 minutes, or until deep golden, then remove from the oven. Add the thyme, olives and almonds, stir well to combine, and season, to taste. Cool slightly.

Use 1½ tablespoons of the oil to grease the base and side of a 26 cm (10½ inch) square ceramic baking dish. Working with one sardine fillet at a time, spoon a scant tablespoon of the crumb mixture along the head end and roll up towards the tail. Place the rolled sardine in the baking dish and repeat until all are rolled. Scatter any remaining crumb mixture over the top and drizzle over the remaining olive oil. Bake the sardines in the oven for 20 minutes, or until they are just cooked through. Serve hot or at room temperature with the potato–garlic purée and lemon wedges passed separately. **SERVES 6–8**

INGREDIENTS

150 ml (5 fl oz) extra virgin olive oil
100 g (3½ oz/1 cup) dry breadcrumbs
1 small onion, finely chopped
2 garlic cloves, crushed
1½ teaspoons sweet paprika
½ teaspoon dried chilli flakes
3 teaspoons thyme leaves
50 g (1¾ oz/⅓ cup) pitted black olives, chopped
80 g (2¾ oz/½ cup) blanched almonds, roasted and chopped
24 butterflied sardine fillets (about 800 g/1 lb 12 oz)
lemon wedges, to serve

POTATO–GARLIC PUREE

450 g (1 lb) all-purpose potatoes, such as desiree, peeled and halved
3–4 garlic cloves, crushed
2½ tablespoons white wine vinegar
125 ml (4 fl oz/½ cup) extra virgin olive oil

HAYAT
CADDESİ

BALIKÇI
DERYA

SWORDFISH KEBABS WITH CELERIAC, ORANGE AND WALNUT SALAD

INGREDIENTS

4 x 200 g (7 oz) skinless, boneless
    swordfish steaks
2 garlic cloves, crushed
250 ml (9 fl oz/1 cup) freshly squeezed
    orange juice
80 ml (2½ fl oz/⅓ cup) extra virgin olive oil
2 tablespoons chopped dill

CELERIAC, ORANGE AND WALNUT SALAD

100 ml (3½ fl oz) freshly squeezed
    orange juice
2 teaspoons finely grated orange zest
600 g (1 lb 5 oz) celeriac, trimmed and peeled
1 garlic clove, crushed
35 g (1¼ oz/⅓ cup) walnuts, chopped
2 oranges, peeled, white pith removed and
    sliced into 5 mm (¼ inch) rounds

METHOD

Soak 12 wooden skewers in water for 30 minutes, then drain well. Cut the swordfish into 3 cm (1¼ inch) pieces. Combine in a bowl with the garlic, orange juice, 60 ml (2 fl oz/¼ cup) of the olive oil and dill and toss to coat. Cover with plastic wrap and refrigerate for 2–3 hours.

To make the celeriac, orange and walnut salad, combine the orange juice and orange zest in a large bowl. Cut the celeriac in half lengthways, finely slice then cut into very fine matchsticks, adding them to the orange juice mixture in the bowl as you go to prevent it from browning — you may need to add a little more juice to coat the celeriac but take care not to add too much or the dressing will be too thin. Add the garlic and walnuts, then season with sea salt and toss well to combine. Just before serving toss through the orange slices.

Preheat a chargrill plate or barbecue grill to medium–high. Drain the fish and thread onto the soaked skewers, brush with the remaining oil and cook the fish, turning often for about 5 minutes, or until just cooked through but still a little pink in the middle. Serve immediately with the salad. **SERVES 4**

SALMON BAKED IN VINE LEAVES WITH GRAPE SAUCE

Preheat the oven to 200°C (400°F/Gas 6). Working with one salmon fillet at a time, wrap a vine leaf around the middle of each, making sure the seam overlaps on the skin side. Set aside.

Put the wine, grape juice, pekmez and cinnamon in a large ovenproof frying pan and bring to the boil. Reduce the heat to medium and simmer for 7–8 minutes, or until the liquid has reduced by half. Carefully add the salmon to the pan in a single layer, seam side down, then tuck the bay leaves around the fish and scatter over the grapes. Bake in the oven for 8–10 minutes, or until the fish is cooked through but still a little pink in the middle. Remove from the oven and serve immediately. **SERVES 6**

12 x 100 g (3½ oz) skinless, boneless salmon fillets

12 large preserved vine leaves, rinsed well and dried

250 ml (9 fl oz/1 cup) red wine

250 ml (9 fl oz/1 cup) grape juice

2½ tablespoons pekmez (see note page 73)

1½ cinnamon sticks, broken

5 fresh bay leaves

360 g (12¾ oz/2 cups) seedless black grapes, halved

POULTRY AND MEAT

Meat features heavily in the Turkish diet; beef and chicken are widely consumed but really, when a Turk says 'meat' he means lamb or mutton. On weekends or long summer evenings, it is not uncommon for Turkish families to pack up their portable *mangal* (charcoal grill), take it to a park or beach and fire it up. Apart from special ceremonies or occasions when a whole animal might be cooked, meat dishes mostly comprise minced or cut-up pieces of flesh cooked with vegetables or fruits, most likely a throwback to the Ottoman era. As an Islamic nation, meat in Turkey must be halal and is always very well cooked.

CHICKEN LIVER KEBABS WITH CHESTNUT PILAF AND RAISIN HOSHAF

METHOD

To make the raisin hoshaf, put the raisins in a bowl and pour over 185 ml (6 fl oz/³/₄ cup) boiling water. Leave to soak for 30 minutes, then place in a saucepan with the soaking liquid over medium–low heat with the sugar. Bring slowly to a simmer and cook for about 15 minutes, or until the liquid is reduced and syrupy. Remove from the heat and cool. Hoshaf will keep indefinitely, stored in an airtight container, in the refrigerator.

Cut each chicken liver into thirds widthways. Combine in a bowl with the garlic, cloves and olive oil, stir to coat well, then cover with plastic wrap and refrigerate for 2–3 hours.

Preheat the oven to 180°C (350°F/Gas 4).

To make the chestnut pilaf, use a small, sharp knife to cut a small cross in the base of each chestnut. Place in a roasting tin and cook for 20 minutes. Cool slightly then, when cool enough to handle, peel the chestnuts to remove the papery layer.

Rinse the bulghur well and then drain. Heat the butter in a saucepan over medium heat. Add the onion and cook for 5–7 minutes, or until softened. Add the rosemary, bulghur and stock, cover, and bring to a simmer. Cook over medium–low heat for 7–8 minutes, or until all the liquid has been absorbed, then quickly add the chestnuts and stir through. Remove from the heat, cover and stand for 15 minutes or until the bulghur is tender. Season with sea salt and freshly ground black pepper, and stir carefully with a fork to fluff the grains.

Meanwhile, drain the chicken livers and thread onto eight metal skewers; season well. Heat a chargrill pan or barbecue grill to medium–high and cook the chicken livers for 5–6 minutes, turning occasionally, until charred on the outside but still a little pink in the middle. Serve immediately with the chestnut pilaf and raisin hoshaf spooned over the top. **SERVES 4**

INGREDIENTS

750 g (1 lb 10 oz) chicken livers, cleaned

3 garlic cloves, crushed

1 large pinch ground cloves

60 ml (2 fl oz/¹/₄ cup) extra virgin olive oil

CHESTNUT PILAF

500 g (1 lb 2 oz) chestnuts

350 g (12 oz/2 cups) coarse bulghur (burgul)

2¹/₂ tablespoons butter

1 onion

2¹/₂ teaspoons chopped rosemary

600 ml (21 fl oz) chicken stock

RAISIN HOSHAF

60 g (2¹/₄ oz/¹/₂ cup) raisins

110 g (3³/₄ oz/¹/₂ cup) caster (superfine) sugar

CHICKEN IN YOGHURT WITH CHOPPED GREEN SALAD

INGREDIENTS

125 g (4½ oz/½ cup) Greek-style yoghurt,
plus extra, to serve

2 teaspoons sweet paprika

1 teaspoon ground cinnamon

1 teaspoon cayenne pepper, or to taste

3 garlic cloves, very finely chopped

2½ tablespoons freshly squeezed lemon juice

2½ tablespoons extra virgin olive oil,
plus extra, for cooking

½ teaspoon freshly ground black pepper

½ onion, coarsely grated

2 x 1 kg (2 lb 4 oz) whole free-range chickens,
each cut into 8 pieces

flat bread (see page 63), to serve

CHOPPED GREEN SALAD

2 garlic cloves, crushed

80 ml (2½ fl oz/⅓ cup) extra virgin olive oil

1 tablespoon freshly squeezed lemon juice

1½ teaspoons caster (superfine) sugar

½ teaspoon dried chilli flakes

4 green tomatoes, cut into 5 mm
(¼ inch) pieces

2 Lebanese (short) cucumbers, cut into
5 mm (¼ inch) pieces

2 green onions (scallions), finely sliced

1 green capsicum (pepper), seeded,
membrane removed and cut into 5 mm
(¼ inch) pieces

¼ cup flat-leaf (Italian) parsley leaves,
chopped

½ cup chopped coriander (cilantro) leaves

METHOD

To prepare the chicken, combine all of the ingredients except the chicken in a large bowl and stir well to combine. Add the chicken pieces and turn to coat, then cover with plastic wrap and refrigerate for 3 hours or overnight.

To make the chopped green salad, combine the garlic, olive oil, lemon juice, sugar and chilli in a bowl. Season with sea salt and freshly ground black pepper, to taste, and whisk well to combine. Combine the remaining ingredients in a large bowl, stir gently, then add the dressing and toss to coat. Set aside.

Drain the chicken and use your hands to remove as much of the marinade as possible. Heat a chargrill pan or barbecue grill to medium. Brush the chicken with olive oil, season with sea salt and freshly ground black pepper, and cook for about 15–20 minutes, turning occasionally, until just cooked through. Serve with the chopped green salad, yoghurt and flat bread passed separately. **SERVES 4**

EGGPLANT AND VEAL TRAY KEBAB

INGREDIENTS

900 g (2 lb/2 large) eggplants (aubergines)

extra virgin olive oil, for cooking

800 g (1 lb 12 oz) minced (ground) veal

2 thick slices day-old rustic bread, crusts
     removed, cut into 5 mm (¼ inch) pieces

1 onion, grated

2 garlic cloves, crushed

2 teaspoons ground cumin

1½ teaspoons sweet paprika

½ teaspoon dried chilli flakes

½ teaspoon sea salt

½ teaspoon freshly ground black pepper

2½ tablespoons chopped oregano leaves

2½ tablespoons chopped flat-leaf (Italian)
     parsley leaves

2 eggs, lightly beaten

125 g (4½ oz) feta cheese, crumbled

250 ml (9 fl oz/1 cup) chicken stock

2 tablespoons Turkish pepper paste
     (see note page 13)

400 g (14 oz/1⅔ cups) tin tomato passata
     (puréed tomatoes)

METHOD

Trim the eggplants, halve them widthways and cut into 2 cm (¾ inch) thick slices. Layer the slices in a colander, sprinkling with salt as you go and set aside for 30 minutes. Rinse well and pat dry with paper towels. Heat a large, heavy-based frying pan over medium heat. Brush the eggplant slices well with olive oil and cook, in batches, for 1–2 minutes on each side, or until light golden. Remove from the pan and set aside.

Preheat the oven to 180°C (350°F/Gas 4).

In a large bowl combine the veal, bread, onion, garlic, cumin, paprika, chilli, salt, pepper, oregano and parsley. Use your hands to knead the mixture until well combined and smooth. Add the egg and mix to combine, then carefully work in the feta, taking care not to break it up too much. Use your hands to form the mixture into balls, about 5 cm (2 inches) round, then flatten slightly into patties. Lay alternating slices of eggplant and meat patties in a large round baking dish. Combine the stock, pepper paste and tomato passata in a bowl and stir to combine. Pour into the dish, then bake in the oven for 1 hour 10 minutes, or until the meat is cooked through. **SERVES 6**

CLOVE AND PINE NUT KÖFTE WITH WHITE BEAN SALAD AND PARSLEY AND TAHINI SAUCE

METHOD

To make the white bean salad, cook the beans in boiling water for 45 minutes or until tender. Drain well, then cool. Meanwhile, toss the sliced onions with the salt in a bowl to combine well, drizzle with the vinegar then stand for 45 minutes or until the onion has softened slightly. Gently stir in the beans, transfer to a bowl and sprinkle with sumac.

To make the parsley and tahini sauce, combine all of the ingredients in a food processor and process until finely chopped. With the motor running, add 125 ml (4 fl oz/¹⁄₂ cup) water, or enough to form a thick creamy sauce. Season with sea salt and freshly ground black pepper, then remove to a bowl and set aside.

To make the clove and pine nut köfte, combine the lamb, breadcrumbs, onion, garlic and spices in the bowl of an electric mixer fitted with a paddle attachment. Mix on medium speed for 5 minutes or until smooth and elastic. Alternatively, you can mix the köfte in a large bowl and knead using your hands for about 10–12 minutes until elastic. Add the pine nuts, season with sea salt and freshly ground black pepper and use your hands to combine.

Take 1 heaped tablespoon of the mixture at a time and form into round oval shapes. Heat 3 tablespoons of the oil in a large, heavy-based frying pan and cook the köfte, in batches, for 7 minutes each, turning often, until deep golden and cooked through. Serve the köfte with the onion and white bean salad and parsley and tahini sauce passed separately. **SERVES 4**

INGREDIENTS

600 g (1 lb 5 oz) minced (ground) lamb
80 g (2³⁄₄ oz/1 cup) fresh breadcrumbs
1 onion, very finely chopped
2 garlic cloves, crushed
³⁄₄ teaspoon ground cloves
¹⁄₂ teaspoon ground allspice
80 g (2³⁄₄ oz/¹⁄₂ cup) pine nuts
125 ml (4 fl oz/¹⁄₂ cup) extra virgin olive oil
rustic bread, to serve
lemon wedges, to serve

PARSLEY AND TAHINI SAUCE

60 ml (2 fl oz/¹⁄₄ cup) tahini
55 ml (1³⁄₄ fl oz) freshly squeezed lemon
    juice, or to taste
¹⁄₂ onion, finely chopped
2 garlic cloves, chopped
125 ml (4 fl oz/¹⁄₂ cup) extra virgin olive oil
2 cups flat-leaf (Italian) parsley leaves
¹⁄₂ teaspoon dried chilli flakes, or to taste

WHITE BEAN SALAD

140 g (5 oz/²⁄₃ cup) dried white beans, soaked
    overnight then drained
2 large red onions, finely sliced
2 teaspoons sea salt
2¹⁄₂ tablespoons red wine vinegar
1¹⁄₂ teaspoons sumac, or to taste

A yahni is a stew made with brown onions and a simple stock base, of which there are many varieties in Turkey. This yahni is best served with a plain pilaf, either rice or burghul, and a fresh green salad.

LAMB, FIG AND ONION YAHNI

METHOD

Soak the figs in 250 ml (9 fl oz/1 cup) boiling water in a small bowl for 45 minutes.

Preheat the oven to 170°C (325°F/Gas 3).

Heat half of the olive oil in a large flameproof casserole dish over medium heat. Add the onion and cook, stirring often, for 15 minutes, or until golden all over. Remove to a bowl.

Dust the lamb lightly in flour, shaking off any excess. Heat the remaining olive oil in the same casserole dish over medium heat. Add the lamb, in batches, and cook for 6 minutes, turning once, until golden all over. Transfer the lamb to the bowl with the onions, then add the tomato paste and allspice to the casserole and cook, stirring, for 1 minute. Stir in the wine, bring to the boil, and cook for 3–4 minutes, or until reduced slightly, then add the stock, figs and any soaking liquid, lamb, onion and bay leaves. Bring to a simmer, cover with a lid, and cook in the oven for 1½ hours, or until the lamb is very tender. Remove the bay leaves and serve with crusty bread. **SERVES 6**

INGREDIENTS

300 g (10½ oz/2 cups) dried figs,
   stems trimmed

100 ml (3½ fl oz) extra virgin olive oil

5 brown onions, peeled leaving root end
   intact, then quartered lengthways

6 lamb forequarter chops, trimmed of excess
   fat and halved

75 g (2¾ oz/½ cup) plain (all-purpose)
   flour, seasoned

2 tablespoons tomato paste
   (concentrated purée)

1 teaspoon ground allspice

250 ml (9 fl oz/1 cup) red wine

125 ml (4 fl oz/½ cup) chicken stock

2 fresh bay leaves

THERE IS MORE THAN ONE WAY TO COOK A KEBAB

I've eaten kebabs all over the country. Every region has its own version of the kebab, which in Turkish simply means 'cooked meat'. Some are so famous they are replicated nationwide, like the spicy, minced Adana kebab. Named after that city, it is a long brochette of minced meat grilled over charcoals. Traditionally the meat for minced kebabs is hand-cut with an enormous, sabre-like knife called a *zirh* — purists claim the finished product won't have the right texture if minced by any other means.

Establishments that make kebabs the slow way using a *zirh* are not so common anymore but do still exist. When I am in Gaziantep I am lucky enough to stumble upon one on Sacir Cardessi, a pedestrian strip cluttered with casual kebab joints. Here they make kebabs using an indigenous fat-tailed sheep called *Helvik* that graze on pastures thick with wild mountain herbs. Great clouds of smoke usher from charcoal-fired grills, over which big meat-laden skewers of kebabs are sizzling. Burly men preside over the cooking, turning the juicy morsels with great care and deftness.

It may not look like it but cooking kebabs is quite a skill. First, a decent kebab needs a judicious amount of lamb fat (about forty per cent) to give it flavour and that unmistakable juiciness. Then the heat source needs to be carefully managed — the meat has to be kept just the right distance away, and then it has to be turned regularly so that the fat melts perfectly at the same time. All the while the juices need to be mopped up with pieces of flat bread as the kebab cooks, so they don't hit the coals and cause flare-up. It requires an incredible amount of concentration and experience to get it right. This is barbecuing elevated to an art form.

Which is why kebabs come in many guises. In Erzurum, I eat cağ kebab, which is constructed of slices of lamb threaded onto a large spit, with a seasoned minced beef mixture layered between to hold it together. The whole thing, which is massive, roasts horizontally over a wood fire and tender, juicy slices are carved off to order. In Malatya, I try the local speciality known as kağit kebab, where slices of meat and vegetables are wrapped in thick, oily paper and baked slowly so all the tasty juices stay inside and infuse everything in their path. In season, they also make an apricot kebab along with the loquat kebab of Gaziantep, and I regret that I am not visiting at the right time of year to try them.

PISTACHIO KEBABS WITH TOMATO CHILLI SAUCE

INGREDIENTS

850 g (1 lb 14 oz) minced (ground) beef

2 tablespoons Turkish pepper paste
　(see note page 13)

3 teaspoons baharat (see note)

1 teaspoon chilli powder

1 egg white

140 g (5 oz/1 cup) pistachios, finely chopped

1 large onion, grated

1½ teaspoons sea salt

1½ teaspoons freshly ground black pepper

200 g (7 oz) small banana peppers

300 g (10½ oz) small, firm, ripe tomatoes

3 red onions, peeled and cut into thick
　wedges, leaving root end intact

olive oil, for cooking

TOMATO CHILLI SAUCE

2 tablespoons olive oil

1 onion, finely chopped

2 garlic cloves, chopped

2 red chillies, finely chopped

2 tablespoons tomato paste
　(concentrated purée)

1 tablespoon sugar

800 g (1 lb 12 oz/3¼ cups) tin chopped
　tomatoes

METHOD

To make the tomato chilli sauce, heat the olive oil in a saucepan over medium heat. Add the onion and garlic and cook for 5–7 minutes, or until softened. Add the chilli and tomato paste, and cook, stirring, for another 2 minutes, then add the sugar and tomato. Bring to a simmer, then reduce the heat to low and cook for 35 minutes, stirring occasionally, until reduced slightly and thickened. Remove from the heat and keep warm.

Combine the beef, pepper paste, baharat and chilli powder in the bowl of an electric mixer fitted with a beater attachment and mix on low speed for 7–8 minutes, or until the mixture is smooth and slightly elastic. Add the egg white, pistachios, onion, salt and pepper. Mix for another 4–5 minutes, or until smooth and slightly sticky. Alternatively, you can mix in a large bowl and knead using your hands for 10–12 minutes until elastic. Divide the mixture into 12 even-sized portions and use your hands to roll each into a sausage shape, about 16 cm (6¼ inches) long. Thread each sausage onto a large, flat metal skewer, then press lightly to flatten.

Preheat a chargrill pan or barbecue grill to medium–high. Brush the vegetables all over with olive oil then chargrill, in batches if necessary, for 6–8 minutes, turning often until charred and tender. Remove to a plate.

Brush the kebabs all over with olive oil and grill, in batches if necessary, for about 3 minutes on each side, or until just cooked through. Serve the kebabs with the tomato chilli sauce and grilled vegetables passed separately. **SERVES 6**

Note: Baharat is a spice mix used in Turkey, as well as throughout the Middle East. Its exact composition varies, but allspice, peppercorns, cloves, cinnamon, cumin and paprika are common, and in Turkey, dried mint is used too. You can by baharat from Middle Eastern grocery stores.

This dish doubtless has its roots in Ottoman cuisine, where the inclusion of fruit and nuts in meat-based dishes was not unusual. This chicken dish with dried apricots and saffron is best served with a sprinkling of chopped pistachios or roasted almonds for an extra layer of richness.

MAHMUDIYE

INGREDIENTS

150 g (5½ oz) dried apricots

1 large pinch saffron threads

25 g (1 oz) butter, chopped

16 small pickling onions, peeled and halved, leaving the root end intact

1.25 kg (2 lb 12 oz) whole free-range chicken, cut into 8 pieces

40 g (1½ oz/⅓ cup) sultanas (golden raisins)

250 ml (9 fl oz/1 cup) chicken stock

1 cinnamon stick

1 tablespoon honey

1 tablespoon freshly squeezed lemon juice

METHOD

Put the apricots in a small bowl and pour over 250 ml (9 fl oz/1 cup) boiling water. Leave to soak for 1 hour, or until softened. Put the saffron in a small bowl with 2 tablespoons hot water and leave to infuse for 30 minutes.

Melt half the butter in a large flameproof casserole dish over medium heat. Add the onion and cook for 6–7 minutes, or until light golden. Remove with a slotted spoon. Add the chicken to the casserole dish and cook for 6 minutes, turning often, until sealed all over. Return the onion to the dish with the apricots and any soaking liquid, the sultanas, stock, saffron liquid, cinnamon and honey; season with sea salt and freshly ground black pepper. Bring to a simmer, then reduce the heat to low, cover, and cook for 35–40 minutes, or until the chicken is tender. Stir in the lemon juice, then divide among serving dishes and serve immediately with boiled potatoes and a green salad passed separately.
SERVES 4

BAHARAT-RUBBED VEAL WITH GRILLED BREAD, PUMPKIN AND FIG SALAD

INGREDIENTS

2 teaspoons baharat (see note page 196)

1 tablespoon plain (all-purpose) flour

1.2 kg (2 lb 10 oz) veal rib roast, trimmed

170 ml (5½ fl oz/⅔ cup) extra virgin olive oil

2½ tablespoons red wine vinegar

3 teaspoons caster (superfine) sugar

700 g (1 lb 9 oz) jap pumpkin (winter squash),
    peeled, seeded and cut into 5 mm
    (¼ inch) slices

6–8 firm, ripe figs, trimmed and
    halved lengthways

6 thick slices rustic bread

150 g (5½ oz) rocket (arugula) leaves

METHOD

Preheat the oven to 180°C (350°F/Gas 4). Combine the baharat and flour in a bowl, season with sea salt and freshly ground black pepper, then rub all over the veal to coat on all sides, shaking off any excess. Heat 1½ tablespoons of the olive oil in a large ovenproof frying pan over medium–high heat. Add the veal and cook, turning often, for 3–4 minutes, or until sealed all over. Transfer the pan to the oven and cook for 35–40 minutes, or until the meat is just cooked through — the veal should still be a little pink in the middle. Remove the pan from the oven, cover loosely with foil and rest for 10 minutes.

Meanwhile, heat a chargrill pan to medium–high. Combine the vinegar and sugar in a small bowl and stir to dissolve the sugar. Set aside. Combine the pumpkin and 80 ml (2½ fl oz/⅓ cup) of the olive oil in a bowl and toss to coat. Grill the pumpkin, in batches, for about 3 minutes on each side or until tender, then remove to a large bowl. Brush the figs with 1 tablespoon of the olive oil and cook, cut side down, for 2 minutes or until slightly softened, then turn over and grill for another 1–2 minutes. Brush the bread all over with the remaining olive oil, then grill for 3 minutes on each side or until lightly charred and crisp, then cool. Using your hands, break the bread slices into coarse pieces and add to the pumpkin and figs in the bowl. Add the rocket and drizzle with the vinegar mixture, then gently toss to combine.

To serve, cut the veal between the bones into four even-sized pieces, then divide among serving plates. Top with the salad mixture and serve immediately.

SERVES 4

EGGPLANT-WRAPPED CHICKEN DRUMSTICKS WITH ROAST CAPSICUM AND ALMONDS

METHOD

Using a large sharp knife, make four or five cuts into each chicken drumstick, cutting nearly down to the bone. Combine the garlic, lemon juice, pepper paste, allspice and 60 ml (2 fl oz/¼ cup) of the olive oil in a large bowl; season with freshly ground black pepper. Add the chicken and toss well to coat, then cover with plastic wrap and refrigerate for 2–3 hours.

Meanwhile, cut the eggplants lengthways into slices about 8 mm (⅜ inch) thick — you will need sixteen slices in total. Layer the eggplant in a colander, sprinkling lightly with salt. Leave to drain for 30 minutes, then rinse well and pat dry with paper towels. Heat 2 tablespoons of the olive oil in a large frying pan and cook the eggplant, in batches, for 3–4 minutes, adding more oil as needed until golden on both sides. Remove to a plate.

Preheat the oven to 180°C (350°F/Gas 4). Place the capsicums in a large baking dish. Drizzle over 2 tablespoons of the olive oil and sprinkle with the sugar. Roast for 35 minutes, or until slightly blackened around the edges. Remove to a bowl and set aside.

Drain the chicken well, reserving the marinade. Heat the remaining olive oil in the same pan over medium–high and cook the chicken for 2–3 minutes, turning once, or until golden all over.

Take two slices of eggplant and lay them on a clean work surface so they slightly overlap. Place a chicken drumstick in the middle, then fold the eggplant over to enclose. Repeat with the remaining eggplant and drumsticks. Place the wrapped drumsticks in a baking dish, then pour over the reserved marinade and chicken stock. Bake the drumsticks in the oven for 35 minutes, or until cooked through. Add the almonds and basil to the capsicums in a bowl and toss to combine. Divide the chicken between serving plates and spoon a little of the pan juices over the top. Serve immediately with the capsicum mixture on the side. **SERVES 4**

INGREDIENTS

8 chicken drumsticks, French-trimmed, skins removed

2 garlic cloves, crushed

60 ml (2 fl oz/¼ cup) freshly squeezed lemon juice

1 tablespoon Turkish pepper paste (see note page 13)

½ teaspoon ground allspice

170 ml (5½ fl oz/⅔ cup) extra virgin olive oil

2 large eggplants (aubergines), trimmed

3 red capsicums (peppers), seeded, membrane removed and cut into 4 cm (1½ inch) pieces

1 tablespoon caster (superfine) sugar

125 ml (4 fl oz/½ cup) chicken stock

50 g (1¾ oz/⅓ cup) blanched almonds, roasted and chopped

¼ cup basil leaves

ROAST GOOSE OF KARS
AND A PITI FIX

I'm not big on tourist sights. But it's a long haul to Kars from anywhere and it would be churlish of me to not visit Ani, the celebrated medieval ruins of the old Armenian capital, forty-five kilometres to the north. It's the main, if not only, reason most tourists visit this town. Thanks to frosty Turkish-Armenian relations and the firmly shut border between the two nations that falls to a river right beside Ani, it's strictly on the road to nowhere.

The ruins at Ani are interesting enough and the trip there makes for a pleasant morning out, but truthfully, I'd rather be scratching around the tree-lined backstreets of Kars. Filled with gorgeous old pastel-hued, neo-classical buildings, a legacy of the Russian control of the city that only ceased in 1918, they're a pleasure to haunt.

'Kar' means 'snow' in Turkish and this place gets desperately cold (about minus 20°C) in winter. This is the season for the goose dishes for which Kars is famous. Geese are reared in the surrounding villages and it is tradition for farmers to kill them in autumn, when they are eight months old. The birds are then salted, dried and stored for winter use. There's a goose market in operation during the winter I'm told, and the birds are expensive, fetching around US$35 each.

After a futile search (most places just tell me to come back in January), I finally find a restaurant, which actually delivers on its promise of *kais var*, or 'we have goose'. The big draw is organic roast goose served on bulghur pilaf with pickles. Once, the bird would have been cooked in a tandoor oven but these days a gas oven does the job spectacularly well, producing rich, gutsy-flavoured meat.

I'm not long in town before I discover that a lot of the meat in Kars is renowned for its deep flavour, and then I stumble upon another local speciality I instantly love: piti. A cross between a soup and a stew, piti is a meal served in two parts. Chunks of lamb, tomatoes and chickpeas are combined with rich meaty stock, spiked with saffron, and then cooked for an age in a large enamel mug. To eat it, the cooking liquid is poured over a bowl of torn lavash and the solids up-ended onto a separate plate.

Apart from the forbidding Kars citadel and the striking old Armenian Church of the Apostles, there's little else to do in Kars, but I'm hardly complaining. While I'm in town I turn up for a piti fix daily.

CIĞ KÖFTE

Using a sharp knife, remove all traces of fat, sinew and connective tissue from the meat or the texture of the köfte will not be smooth. Using a meat grinder, mince the meat three times, or until very finely minced. Alternatively, cut the meat into 1 cm (½ inch) pieces, then place in a food processor and using the pulse button, process the meat until very finely minced.

Place the burghul in a bowl and add enough cold water to just cover, then leave to soak for 10 minutes. Drain well in a fine sieve, pressing with your hands to remove as much liquid as possible.

Place the minced meat in the bowl of an electric mixture fitted with a paddle attachment. Add the burghul, tomato, onion, garlic, pepper paste, tomato paste, pomegranate molasses, allspice, cumin, chilli, parsley and coriander. Mix on low speed for 10 minutes, or until the mixture is smooth and a little elastic; season with sea salt and freshly ground black pepper. Alternatively, you can mix the köfte in a large bowl and knead using your hands for 10–12 minutes until elastic.

To serve, smear some of the köfte mixture onto the flatbread and serve with a drizzle of lemon juice squeezed over. **SERVES 6**

750 g (1 lb 10 oz) lamb rump

250 g (9 oz) fine burghul (bulgur)

2 tomatoes, coarsely grated

1 large onion, finely grated

2 garlic cloves, crushed

1½ tablespoons Turkish pepper paste
    (see note page 13)

1 tablespoon tomato paste
    (concentrated purée)

1½ tablespoons pomegranate molasses
    (see note page 25)

½ teaspoon ground allspice

2 teaspoons ground cumin

2 teaspoons dried chilli flakes, or to taste

1 cup flat-leaf (Italian) parsley leaves,
    chopped

1 cup coriander (cilantro) leaves, chopped

flat bread (see page 63), to serve

lemon wedges, to serve

BAKED RABBIT WITH CINNAMON RICE AND LEMON SAUCE

INGREDIENTS

1.6 kg (3 lb 8 oz) farmed rabbit, cut into
    8 pieces (ask your butcher to do this)
2 tablespoons extra virgin olive oil
3 garlic cloves, crushed
165 g (5¾ oz) thinly sliced pastirma
    (see note) (optional)
3 fresh bay leaves
100 ml (3½ fl oz) dry white wine

CINNAMON RICE

2 tablespoons olive oil
1 large onion, finely chopped
2 garlic cloves, crushed
60 g (2¼ oz/½ cup) sultanas (golden raisins)
35 g (1¼ oz/⅓ cup) walnuts, chopped
1½ teaspoons ground cinnamon
300 g (10½ oz/1½ cups) long-grain white rice
600 ml (21 fl oz) chicken stock

LEMON SAUCE

1 tablespoon cornflour (cornstarch)
500 ml (17 fl oz/2 cups) chicken stock
100 ml (3½ fl oz) freshly squeezed
    lemon juice
4 egg yolks, lightly beaten
1½ teaspoons finely grated lemon zest

METHOD

Preheat the oven to 180°C (350°F/Gas 4).

To prepare the rabbit, combine the olive oil and garlic together in a bowl. Place the rabbit pieces in a single layer in a large baking dish and rub over the garlic oil mixture to coat. Season with sea salt and freshly ground black pepper, then lay pastirma slices over, if using, slightly overlapping, to cover the rabbit pieces. Add the bay leaves and wine, cover tightly with foil, and bake for 50–60 minutes, or until the rabbit is tender. Remove the dish from the oven and stand for 10 minutes.

To make the lemon sauce, combine the cornflour in a small bowl with just enough of the chicken stock to form a smooth paste. Combine the remaining stock and lemon juice in a small saucepan and bring to the boil. Whisking constantly, add the cornflour paste and bring to the boil, stirring until the mixture thickens slightly. Remove from the heat and cool slightly. Combine the egg yolks in a small bowl with 125 ml (4 fl oz/½ cup) of the stock mixture and stir until smooth, then return to the stock in the pan and, whisking constantly, cook over medium heat for about 3 minutes, or until the sauce thickens enough to coat the back of a spoon — do not allow it to boil or it will curdle. Stir in the lemon zest, season to taste, and keep warm until ready to serve.

Meanwhile, make the cinnamon rice. Heat the olive oil in a large flameproof casserole dish over medium heat. Add the onion and garlic and cook for 5–6 minutes, or until softened and lightly browned. Add the sultanas, walnuts, cinnamon and rice and cook, stirring, for 2 minutes. Add the stock, season with sea salt and freshly ground black pepper, bring to the boil and cook for 15 minutes, or until the liquid has been absorbed. Remove from the heat and stand, covered, for 5–10 minutes.

Serve the rabbit with the cinnamon rice, lemon sauce and a green salad passed separately. **SERVES 4–6**

Note: Pastirma is a preserved meat made by salting and air-drying beef, which is then covered with an intensely flavoured spice paste made from cumin, fenugreek, garlic and paprika.

POACHED KÖFTE IN LEMON SAUCE

INGREDIENTS

1.5 litres (52 fl oz/6 cups) chicken stock

100 g (3½ oz/½ cup) long-grain white rice

600 g (1 lb 5 oz) minced (ground) lamb

1½ teaspoons ground cumin

1 teaspoon sea salt

1 teaspoon freshly ground black pepper

¼ cup flat-leaf (Italian) parsley leaves,
   chopped

2 egg yolks, plus 2 extra for the sauce

2 tablespoons plain (all-purpose) flour

60 ml (2 fl oz/¼ cup) freshly squeezed
   lemon juice

1½ teaspoons finely grated lemon zest

METHOD

Bring the chicken stock to a simmer in a large saucepan over low heat, cover and hold at a gentle simmer until needed.

Put the rice in a bowl and pour over enough boiling water to just cover. Leave to soak for 5 minutes, then drain well and return to the bowl with the lamb, cumin, salt, pepper and parsley. Use your hands to knead the mixture together until smooth and slightly elastic, then add the egg yolks and mix well to combine. Take 1 heaped tablespoon of the mixture at a time and form them into small balls, about the size of a large chestnut. Add the balls slowly to the gently simmering stock. Cook the köfte over low heat for about 20 minutes, or until just cooked through, skimming off any impurities that rise to the surface — do not let the water simmer too rapidly or the köfte will be tough. Remove from the stock using a slotted spoon and set aside. Strain the stock through a fine sieve and return it to the pan.

In a small bowl combine the flour with 2 tablespoons water and stir to combine. Add the extra egg yolks, lemon juice and lemon zest and whisk until smooth. Add 250 ml (9 fl oz/1 cup) of the hot stock and stir to combine. Bring the stock in the saucepan back to a simmer then, stirring constantly, add the flour mixture. Bring to a simmer over medium heat, stirring constantly to avoid lumps forming and cook for 5 minutes, or until the mixture has thickened. Return the köfte to the pan and cook gently for 3–4 minutes to heat through. Divide among bowls and serve immediately with crusty bread and a green salad passed separately. **SERVES 4**

SPATCHCOCKS WITH SPICED WHEAT STUFFING, PLUMS AND PEKMEZ GLAZE

METHOD

To make the spiced wheat stuffing, place the burghul in a bowl and add enough cold water to just cover, then leave to soak for 10 minutes. Drain well in a fine sieve, pressing with your hands to remove as much liquid as possible.

Meanwhile, heat the butter in a saucepan over medium heat. Add the onion and garlic and cook for 5–7 minutes, or until softened. Add the allspice and cinnamon and cook for 1 minute, stirring, until fragrant. Remove from the heat and stir in the hazelnuts, then cool to room temperature. Combine the onion mixture with the burghul, chicken and coriander in a large bowl, season with sea salt and freshly ground black pepper, then stir well to combine.

Preheat the oven to 180°C (350°F/Gas 4) and lightly grease a large baking dish. Working with one spatchcock at a time, fill the cavity with the spiced wheat stuffing and secure each opening with a toothpick. Tie the legs together with kitchen string to secure. Arrange the spatchcocks in the prepared dish, breast side down. Combine the pekmez and red wine and drizzle over the spatchcocks to coat. Season with sea salt and freshly ground black pepper and cook in the oven for 45 minutes. Turn the spatchcocks over, add the plums to the dish, and continue cooking for 20 minutes, or until the spatchcocks and stuffing are cooked through and the plums are tender. Remove the kitchen string and toothpicks and serve the spatchcocks and plums with any pan juices spooned over the top and a green salad passed separately. **SERVES 4**

INGREDIENTS

2 tablespoons olive oil

4 x 400 g (14 oz) spatchcocks (poussin), trimmed and giblets removed

80 ml (2½ fl oz/⅓ cup) pekmez (see note page 73)

60 ml (2 fl oz/¼ cup) red wine

6 large, firm, ripe freestone plums, halved, stones removed

SPICED WHEAT STUFFING

125 g (4½ oz/¾ cup) coarse burghul (bulgur)

25 g (1 oz) unsalted butter

1 onion, finely chopped

1 garlic clove, crushed

½ teaspoon ground allspice

½ teaspoon ground cinnamon

70 g (2½ oz/½ cup) hazelnuts, roasted, peeled and chopped

350 g (12 oz) minced (ground) chicken

1 cup coriander (cilantro) leaves, chopped

This slow-roasted lamb is terrific served with the burghul pilaf on page 140, especially with a few handfuls of torn mint leaves stirred through the burghul just before serving.

SLOW-ROASTED LAMB WITH APPLES POACHED IN POMEGRANATE

METHOD

Preheat the oven to 150°C (300°F/Gas 2). Trim any excess fat from the leg of lamb.

Combine the butter, paprika, cumin, cinnamon, salt and pepper in a bowl. Smear the butter mixture over the lamb, then wrap the leg in foil or baking paper and place in a baking dish. Bake the lamb in the oven for 6–7 hours, or until the meat is falling from the bone.

About an hour before the lamb has finished cooking, start preparing the apples. Combine the walnuts, raisins, allspice, dried mint and pomegranate molasses in a small bowl and mix well. Divide the mixture among the apple cavities until well filled. Place the apples in a saucepan side by side so they fit snugly in a single layer, then add the honey and pomegranate juice. Cover the pan, bring slowly to a simmer, and cook over low heat for about 40 minutes, or until the apples are tender.

To serve, pull the lamb apart into chunks and serve with the apples on the side and some of the pomegranate mixture spooned over. **SERVES 6**

INGREDIENTS

2.5 kg (5 lb 8 oz) leg of lamb

100 g (3½ oz) softened butter

2 teaspoons paprika

1½ teaspoons ground cumin

1 teaspoon ground cinnamon

1 teaspoon sea salt

1 teaspoon freshly ground black pepper

40 g (1½ oz/⅓ cup) chopped walnut pieces

40 g (1½ oz/⅓ cup) chopped white raisins
(see note page 134) or sultanas
(golden raisins)

½ teaspoon ground allspice

1½ teaspoon dried mint

1 tablespoon pomegranate molasses
(see note page 25)

6 small granny smith apples, peeled
and cored

2 tablespoons honey

500 ml (17 fl oz/2 cups) pomegranate juice

LAMB CHOPS BAKED IN PAPER WITH POTATOES, LEMON, MINT AND OLIVES

INGREDIENTS

6 lamb neck chops (about 1.5 kg/3 lb 5 oz)

2 tablespoons olive oil

3 garlic cloves, finely chopped

60 ml (2 fl oz/¼ cup) extra virgin olive oil

600 g (1 lb 5 oz) kipfler potatoes, peeled and halved if large

600 g (1 lb 5 oz) unripe red tomatoes, cut into thick wedges

2 teaspoons dried mint

1½ teaspoons cumin seeds

1 lemon, thinly slice

60 g (2¼ oz/½ cup) Ligurian or other small olives

METHOD

Preheat the oven to 160°C (315°F/Gas 2–3). Cut each chop in half using the natural lines of the meat as a guide, then remove any excess fat. Cut six 30 cm (12 inch) squares of baking paper.

Heat 1 tablespoon of the olive oil in a large frying pan over medium–high heat. Add the lamb and cook for 1–2 minutes on each side, or until browned all over. Remove from the heat. Working with one sheet of paper at a time, place two pieces of lamb in the centre of each, season with sea salt and freshly ground black pepper and sprinkle over a little of the garlic. Bring two opposite sides of the paper together over the top of the meat and fold several times to seal. Fold the other sides over the meat to form a tight package, then use small metal skewers to seal each parcel. Set aside.

Peel the potatoes and cut them into quarters lengthways, then place into a roasting dish with the tomato. Drizzle with the remaining oil, scatter over the mint, cumin seeds, remaining garlic and lemon slices and season well with salt and pepper. Toss to coat the vegetables and cook in the oven for 30 minutes, then tuck the lamb parcels in among the potato mixture. Scatter over the olives and cook for another 20–30 minutes, or until the lamb is cooked through and the vegetables are tender. Remove from the oven, cover the dish with foil, and rest the meat for 10 minutes before serving. Serve the lamb in the paper with the potato mixture to the side. **SERVES 6**

ROAST CARROT, VEAL AND LEMON-SCENTED MOUSSAKA

INGREDIENTS

1.2 kg (2 lb 10 oz) carrots, cut into 5 mm
  ($\frac{1}{4}$ inch) thick batons
100 ml ($3\frac{1}{2}$ fl oz) olive oil
2 onions, finely chopped
3 garlic cloves, finely chopped
600 g (1 lb 5 oz) minced (ground) veal
$2\frac{1}{2}$ tablespoons tomato paste
  (concentrated purée)
1 teaspoon ground allspice
35 g ($1\frac{1}{4}$ oz/$\frac{1}{4}$ cup) currants
400 g (14 oz/$1\frac{2}{3}$ cups) tin chopped tomatoes

SAUCE

600 ml (21 fl oz) full-cream (whole) milk
50 g ($1\frac{3}{4}$ oz) butter
50 g ($1\frac{3}{4}$ oz /$\frac{1}{3}$ cup) plain (all-purpose) flour
1 teaspoon finely grated lemon zest
$1\frac{1}{2}$ tablespoons chopped oregano
2 egg yolks, beaten

METHOD

To make the sauce, put the milk in a small saucepan and bring to simmering point, then remove from the heat. Melt the butter in a separate saucepan over medium–low heat, then add the flour and cook, stirring, for 2 minutes. Add the milk, 125 ml (4 fl oz/$\frac{1}{2}$ cup) at a time, stirring constantly and bringing back to a simmer between each addition. Reduce the heat and cook the sauce for about 7–8 minutes, stirring often to prevent lumps forming. Remove from the heat and cool slightly, stirring occasionally to prevent a skin forming. Stir in the lemon zest, oregano and egg yolk, season with sea salt and freshly ground black pepper, then cover the surface directly with plastic wrap or baking paper to prevent a skin forming.

Preheat the oven to 180°C (350°F/Gas 4). Combine the carrots in a large bowl with 80 ml ($2\frac{1}{2}$ fl oz/$\frac{1}{3}$ cup) of the olive oil, tossing to coat well. Divide between two large baking dishes and cook in the oven for 40–50 minutes, or until deep golden; strain off any excess oil if necessary.

Meanwhile, heat the remaining oil in a large saucepan over medium heat. Add the onion and garlic and cook for 5–7 minutes, or until softened. Add the veal and cook for 5–6 minutes, stirring to break up any lumps, until it changes colour. Add the tomato paste and cook, stirring for 1 minute, then add the allspice, currants and tomato. Bring to a simmer and cook for 10 minutes. Season with sea salt and freshly ground black pepper.

Scatter half of the roast carrots in the base of a 26 x 22 cm ($10\frac{1}{2}$ x $8\frac{1}{2}$ inch) baking dish. Pour over half of the meat mixture and scatter over the remaining carrots, then use the remaining meat to create an even layer and carefully spread over the sauce. Bake in the oven for 45 minutes, or until the top is golden and the mixture is bubbling. Serve hot with a green salad passed separately.
SERVES 6

VINE-WRAPPED GRILLED QUAILS WITH OLIVE, WALNUT AND POMEGRANATE RELISH

METHOD

Using a large sharp knife, cut through each quail on either side of the backbone and remove the backbone. Cut each quail lengthways between the breastbones. Combine the olive oil, lemon juice, garlic, cumin and pepper in a large bowl and whisk well. Add the quails and toss to coat. Cover with plastic wrap and refrigerate for 3–4 hours. Drain the quails, discarding the marinade.

Meanwhile, soak 12 wooden skewers in water for 30 minutes to prevent them from burning during cooking.

To make the olive, walnut and pomegranate relish, combine all of the ingredients in a bowl and stir well. Season with sea salt and freshly ground black pepper, and set aside until needed.

Place a vine leaf on a work surface, trimming off the tough stem end if necessary. Place a quail half on each leaf, pushing the breast and leg together slightly to form a neat shape, and wrap the vine leaf around the quail. Repeat with the remaining quail halves and vine leaves, then use two skewers to skewer two of the quail halves together. Heat a chargrill pan or barbecue grill to medium–high. Gently brush the wrapped quails all over with oil, and cook in batches, for 10–15 minutes, turning often, until just cooked through — take care not to overcook the quails or they will be dry (they should still be a little pink in the middle).

Divide the quails between serving plates and spoon the relish alongside. Scatter over the coriander sprigs and pomegranate seeds, if using, and serve with the yoghurt and flat bread passed separately. **SERVES 6**

INGREDIENTS

6 x 200 g (7 oz) whole quails

125 ml (4 fl oz/$^1/_2$ cup) olive oil, plus extra, for cooking

2$^1/_2$ tablespoons freshly squeezed lemon juice

2 garlic cloves, crushed

1 teaspoon ground cumin

1 teaspoon freshly ground black pepper

12 large preserved vine leaves, rinsed well and dried

coriander (cilantro) sprigs, to serve

pomegranate seeds, to serve (optional)

Greek-style yoghurt, to serve

flat bread (see page 63), to serve

OLIVE, WALNUT AND POMEGRANATE RELISH

125 g (4$^1/_2$ oz/1 cup) pitted green olives, chopped

100 g (3$^1/_2$ oz/1 cup) walnut halves, chopped

80 ml (2$^1/_2$ fl oz/$^1/_3$ cup) olive oil

1 garlic clove, crushed

1 small red onion, finely chopped

1$^1/_2$ tablespoons pomegranate molasses (see note page 25)

1 tablespoon freshly squeezed lemon juice

$^1/_4$ cup flat-leaf (Italian) parsley leaves

LAMB SHANKS WITH LETTUCE, CHICKPEAS AND MINTED YOGHURT

INGREDIENTS

220 g (7³/₄ oz/1 cup) dried chickpeas, soaked
    overnight and drained

1¹/₂ tablespoons butter

16 small pickling onions, peeled with root
    end left intact

1¹/₂ tablespoons plain (all-purpose) flour

875 ml (30 fl oz/3¹/₂ cups) chicken stock

4 large lamb shanks, French-trimmed

3 thyme sprigs

1 fresh bay leaf

2 teaspoons finely grated lemon zest

2 tablespoons freshly squeezed lemon juice,
    or to taste

2 baby cos (romaine) lettuces, leaves then cut
    into quarters lengthways

MINTED YOGHURT

375 g (13 oz/1¹/₂ cups) Greek-style yoghurt

2¹/₂ tablespoons finely chopped mint, or
    to taste

METHOD

Put the chickpeas in a saucepan and add enough boiling water to just cover, then bring to a simmer and cook over medium heat for about 45 minutes, or until tender. Drain well.

Preheat the oven to 160°C (315°F/Gas 2–3). Melt the butter in a large frying pan over medium heat. Add the onions and cook, shaking the pan often, for 3–4 minutes, or until light golden. Transfer the onions to a large casserole dish using a slotted spoon. Add the flour to the pan and stir into the pan juices for 2–3 minutes. Add the stock, a little at a time, whisking constantly and bringing the mixture to a simmer between each addition. Add the lamb shanks to the casserole dish, pour over the stock, then add the thyme and bay leaf. Cover with a tight-fitting lid, then cook in the oven for 50 minutes. Stir in the lemon zest and lemon juice, then add the chickpeas and lettuce and cook for another 45 minutes, or until the meat is very tender.

To make the minted yoghurt, combine the yoghurt and mint in a bowl, season with sea salt and freshly ground black pepper and stir well to combine. Serve the lamb shanks with the lettuce, chickpeas and some of the sauce spooned over the top, with the minted yoghurt passed separately. **SERVES 4**

Ali nazik is a type of kebab that originated in Gaziantep but is now a popular dish all over Turkey. The addition of sautéed onions is breaking from tradition, but tastes terrific even so. Do try to chop your own meat from scratch and resist the temptation to use minced (ground) lamb.

ALI NAZIK WITH ROCKET AND PARSLEY SALAD

METHOD

Place the eggplants directly over a low flame and cook, turning often, for about 20 minutes or until the skin is blackened all over and the centres are soft. (Alternatively, cook the eggplants on a barbecue grill heated to high.) Transfer the eggplants to a large bowl and cool slightly. When cool enough to handle, peel off the skins, removing as much of the blackened skin as possible and trim the stem end. Transfer the flesh to a colander and drain for about 20 minutes to remove any excess liquid. Finely chop the eggplant then combine in a bowl with the garlic and yoghurt. Season with sea salt and freshly ground black pepper, then set aside.

Use a sharp knife to chop the meat as finely as you can so it resembles minced lamb. Heat half of the butter in a large frying pan over medium heat. Add the onion and cook for about 12 minutes, stirring often, until golden. Remove the onion to a bowl. Melt the remaining butter in the same pan over medium–high heat, add the lamb and cook for about 20 minutes, stirring with a wooden spoon to break up the meat, until well browned. Drain off any excess fat, leaving 2–3 tablespoons in the pan with the meat. Add the paprika, chilli and cumin seeds, if using, and cook, stirring, for another 1 minute, or until fragrant; season with sea salt and freshly ground black pepper.

To make the rocket and parsley salad, combine the parsley, rocket, lemon juice and olive oil in a bowl and toss well to combine.

Divide the eggplant mixture among plates, top with the lamb mixture, then place the onion over the top. Serve immediately with the rocket and parsley salad passed separately. **SERVES 4**

INGREDIENTS

1 kg (2 lb 4 oz) eggplants (aubergines)

2 garlic cloves, crushed

375 g (13 oz/1½ cups) Greek-style yoghurt

800 g (1 lb 12 oz) lamb neck fillet or shoulder, trimmed

50 g (1¾ oz) butter

2 large onions, finely sliced

2 teaspoons sweet paprika

½ teaspoon dried chilli flakes, or to taste

½ teaspoon cumin seeds (optional)

ROCKET AND PARSLEY SALAD

1 cup flat-leaf (Italian) parsley leaves, chopped

100 g (3½ oz/3 cups) rocket (arugula) leaves

2 tablespoons freshly squeezed lemon juice

60 ml (2 fl oz/¼ cup) extra virgin olive oil

DESSERTS

With their fondness for milk puddings, fruit compotes, syrup-drenched cakes, sticky fritters, baklava and the world-famous Turkish delight, the Turkish sweet tooth is legendary. Feasting one's eyes on a street vendor serving the intriguingly stretchy ice cream made using *salep*, or polishing off a selection of baklava, gleaming with syrup and packed with vivid green pistachios, is a highlight of any visit to Turkey. Heady with the flavours of rose, saffron, cinnamon, vanilla, pomegranate, nuts and loads of fruits, both fresh and dried, Turkish desserts are seriously difficult to resist.

I first tried this dish at a trendy canteen in an upmarket precinct in Istanbul where it was served with ice cream — it is one of those dishes that is seemingly artless but its sum is larger than its parts. The trick is to stir and toast the semolina carefully — cooked too slowly and it won't toast, cooked too quickly and it will burn and become bitter.

IRMIK HELVASI

METHOD

To make the sweetened apricots, place the apricots in a bowl with 375 ml (13 fl oz/1½ cups) water — the apricots should be just covered. Set aside for 1 hour, or until the apricots have softened. Place the apricots and soaking water in a saucepan over low heat. Add the sugar and simmer for 15–20 minutes, or until the apricots are very tender. Remove from the heat, set aside and cool.

Stir the milk and sugar in a saucepan over medium–low heat until the sugar has dissolved. Remove from the heat.

Melt the butter in a saucepan over medium–low heat. Add the semolina and cook for about 15 minutes, stirring constantly, until the semolina smells lightly toasted and biscuity and has turned a shade darker. Add the milk mixture, taking care as the mixture may spit, and stir vigorously until combined and smooth. Add the pine nuts and continue cooking over medium–low heat for 2–3 minutes, or until smooth. Cover the pan and cook for 4–5 minutes, or until very thick. Remove from the heat then stand, covered, until cooled to room temperature. Fluff with a fork to separate into small clumps, then serve in bowls with the apricots and whipped cream spooned over the semolina. **SERVES 6**

INGREDIENTS

500 ml (17 fl oz/2 cups) full-cream (whole) milk
220 g (7¾ oz/1 cup) caster (superfine) sugar
100 g (3½ oz) unsalted butter
125 g (4½ oz/1 cup) coarse semolina
40 g (1½ oz/¼ cup) pine nuts, toasted
whipped cream, to serve

SWEETENED APRICOTS

185 g (6½ oz/1 cup) dried apricots
110 g (3¾ oz/½ cup) caster (superfine) sugar

CHERRY BREAD PUDDING WITH ALMOND CREAM

INGREDIENTS

900 g (2 lb) cherries, pitted

375 ml (13 fl oz/1½ cups) sour cherry juice

220 g (7¾ oz/1 cup) caster (superfine) sugar

butter, for spreading

6 x 1 cm (½ inch) thick slices day-old rustic
    bread, crusts trimmed

50 g (1¾ oz/½ cup) flaked almonds,
    toasted

ALMOND CREAM

250 g (9 oz/1 cup) mascarpone

125 ml (4 fl oz/½ cup) pouring
    (whipping) cream

2 tablespoons icing (confectioners') sugar

¼ teaspoon natural almond extract

METHOD

To make the almond cream, combine the mascarpone, cream, icing sugar and almond extract in a bowl and stir well to combine. Cover loosely with plastic wrap and refrigerate until needed.

To make the pudding, combine the cherries, juice and sugar in a saucepan over medium heat and bring slowly to a simmer, gently stirring to dissolve the sugar. Cook for 3–4 minutes, or until the cherries are just tender and have given up their juices. Remove from the heat and cool.

Preheat the oven to 180°C (350°F/Gas 4). Lightly butter the bread, then lay on a baking tray in a single layer and bake for 10–15 minutes, or until golden and crisp.

When ready to serve, divide the bread between deep bowls and spoon the cherry mixture over the top. Serve with the almond cream and toasted flaked almonds. **SERVES 6**

PISTACHIO-SEMOLINA CAKE

To make the syrup, combine the sugar and 125 ml (4 fl oz/$^1/_2$ cup) water in a saucepan and slowly bring to a simmer. Add the cinnamon then simmer over medium heat for 6–7 minutes, or until reduced and slightly thickened. Remove from the heat and stir through the lemon juice, then cool to room temperature. Discard the cinnamon and set aside.

Preheat the oven to 170°C (325°F/Gas 3) and lightly grease and flour a rectangular 25 x 14 cm (10 x 5$^1/_2$ inch) cake tin. Combine the pistachios and sugar in a food processor and process until a fine powder forms. Sift the flour and baking powder into a bowl, then stir in the semolina and pistachio mixture. Combine the milk and butter in a bowl and add to the flour mixture, stirring until smooth. Pour into the prepared dish, smoothing the surface. Bake in the oven for 35 minutes, or until a skewer inserted into the centre of the cake comes out clean. Remove from the oven and pour over the cooled syrup. Stand until the syrup has been absorbed, then cut the cake into 8 cm (3$^1/_4$ inch) diamond shapes and remove from the tin. Sprinkle over the rose petals, if using, and serve.

SERVES 8– 10

INGREDIENTS

100 g (3$^1/_2$ oz/$^3/_4$ cup) pistachios

220 g (7$^3/_4$ oz/1 cup) caster (superfine) sugar

75 g (2$^3/_4$ oz/$^1/_2$ cup) plain (all-purpose) flour

1$^1/_4$ teaspoons baking powder

250 g (9 oz/2 cups) fine semolina

310 ml (10$^3/_4$ fl oz/1$^1/_4$ cups) full-cream (whole) milk

125 g (4$^1/_2$ oz) butter, melted and cooled

2$^1/_2$ tablespoons dried rose petals, to decorate (optional)

SYRUP

220 g (7$^3/_4$ oz/1 cup) caster (superfine) sugar

1 cinnamon stick

2$^1/_2$ tablespoons freshly squeezed lemon juice

ALMOND MILK PUDDING WITH SUGARED ROSE PETALS

INGREDIENTS

1 litre (35 fl oz/4 cups) full-cream (whole) milk

155 g (5½ oz/1 cup) blanched almonds

145 g (5 oz/⅔ cup) caster (superfine) sugar

45 g (1¾ oz/¼ cup) rice flour

200 ml (7 fl oz) pouring (whipping) cream, whipped

2 tablespoons chopped toasted almonds

SUGARED ROSE PETALS

1 egg white

36 petals from fragrant, unsprayed roses

220 g (7¾ oz/1 cup) caster (superfine) sugar

METHOD

To make the sugared rose petals, whisk the egg white well in a bowl. Working with one petal at a time, carefully paint each petal with egg white using a paintbrush, then gently dust in the sugar, shaking off any excess. Place the petals on a fine wire rack overnight so they completely dry out. Sugared rose petals should not be made when the weather is very humid. They will keep, stored in an airtight container, between layers of baking paper, at room temperature for 2–3 days.

Put 875 ml (30 fl oz/3½ cups) of the milk in a saucepan over medium heat and bring almost to a simmer; keep warm. Combine the almonds and sugar in a food processor and process until a very fine powder forms. Combine the rice flour with the remaining milk in a small bowl and mix until smooth. Stirring constantly, add the almond mixture and the rice flour mixture to the milk on the stove. Very slowly bring the mixture to a simmer, stirring constantly to prevent lumps forming, and cook over medium–low heat for 5 minutes, or until thick and smooth. Remove from the heat and cool to room temperature, stirring occasionally to prevent a skin forming. Divide the mixture between six 250 ml (9 fl oz/1 cup) capacity glasses or bowls, then cover each glass with plastic wrap and chill for at least 4 hours before serving.

When you are ready to serve, top each pudding with a dollop of cream and sprinkle over some of the almonds. Scatter over the sugared rose petals and serve immediately. **SERVES 6**

WALNUT-STUFFED FIGS IN RED WINE AND CLOVE SYRUP WITH HONEY ICE CREAM

METHOD

To make the honey ice cream, combine the milk and cream in a saucepan over medium–low heat and bring almost to a simmer, then remove from the heat. Combine the egg yolks and honey in a bowl and, using electric beaters, whisk until thickened. Pour the hot milk mixture over the yolk mixture, stirring well with a wooden spoon to combine. Return the mixture to a clean saucepan and cook over medium–low heat for 6–7 minutes, stirring constantly, until the mixture thickens and coats the back of the spoon — do not allow the mixture to get too hot or it will curdle. Remove from the heat and cool to room temperature, cover and chill. Transfer to an ice-cream machine and churn according to the manufacturer's instructions. Alternatively, transfer to a shallow metal tray and freeze, whisking every couple of hours until frozen and creamy. Honey ice cream will keep in an airtight container for up to 1 week.

Put the figs in a bowl and pour over enough boiling water to just cover. Stand for 4 hours, or overnight, then drain, reserving any liquid. Using a small, sharp knife, cut a small pocket in each fig, just large enough to fit a walnut half. Stuff each fig with a walnut half.

Put the sugar, wine and cloves in a saucepan. Add any reserved fig liquid, plus enough water to make it up to 125 ml (4 fl oz/½ cup) if necessary (or just add the full measure of water). Bring to a simmer, stirring occasionally to dissolve the sugar. Cover the pan and cook over low heat for 10 minutes. Remove the cloves and add the stuffed figs to the syrup. Bring to a simmer over low heat and cook the figs, uncovered, for 25 minutes, or until tender. Cool the figs in the syrup, then serve with the honey ice cream. **SERVES 6**

INGREDIENTS

375 g (13 oz) dried figs, tough stems trimmed
50 g (1¾ oz/½ cup) walnut halves
220 g (7¾ oz/1 cup) caster (superfine) sugar
375 ml (13 fl oz/1½ cups) red wine
6 whole cloves

HONEY ICE CREAM

375 ml (13 fl oz/1½ cups) full-cream (whole) milk
375 ml (13 fl oz/1½ cups) pouring (whipping) cream
6 egg yolks
260 g (9¼ oz/¾ cup) honey

THE CELEBRATED
BAKLAVA OF GAZIANTEP

Within Turkey, Gaziantep is fabled for its cuisine. It has the reputation for being home to the best ali nazik kebabs, the best kadaif, the best lahmacun ... in fact, the best you-name-it. The city is the sixth largest in the country; it's large, modern and vibrant, with a decently preserved historic core. Beyond the city limits are fertile plains producing a cornucopia of produce — pomegranates, stone fruits, mulberries, grapes, sugar beet, wheat and olives, to name but a few. However, the most celebrated crop is the *fistic*, or pistachio. It's said the pistachios grown here and the baklava that's made with them are the best in the world. If that's not an inducement to visit a city then I don't know what is!

To see how baklava is made is an unforgettable sight. At Imam Çağdaş, one of the largest factories in the city, I am lucky enough to watch the baklava-making process at work. And it is amazing, not least because it is largely a completely manual one. Two men bend over a table heaped with shelled pistachios, sorting them by hand to discard those that aren't perfect. In a room thick with flour, a dozen or so men roll out gossamer-thin sheets of dough using special pins; traditionally pear wood is said to produce the best effect. The flour comes from the Harran Plain near Urfa and is tougher than regular flour, allowing the dough to be rolled so super-thin I can read a business card through it. The rolled pastry is then layered into large round tins and after about the fifteenth layer, minced nuts are spread over, then more layers of pastry. It's cut into shapes using a large knife, then hot sheep's milk butter goes over the top. The baklava is baked in wood-fired ovens (oak wood produces the best result) and it is judged ready when the pastry is puffed, golden and crisp, and the pistachios are bright green. While the cooked pastry is still hot, sugar syrup is carefully ladled over the top — a crucial step as uneven distribution of syrup, or the wrong ratio of syrup to pastry, is said to ruin the finished product.

There are some eleven steps involved in making baklava and it takes up to twenty years to become thoroughly expert in them all. I leave Imam Çağdaş gob-smacked at the skill and concentration required to make it and vow not to include a recipe for it in this book. 'Proper' baklava just can't be replicated at home — you have to go to Gaziantep to experience the real thing ...

CHILLED YOGHURT CREAM WITH SWEET TOMATO COMPOTE

INGREDIENTS

2 teaspoons powdered gelatine

300 ml (10½ fl oz) pouring
(whipping) cream

110 g (3¾ oz/½ cup) caster (superfine) sugar

500 g (1 lb 2 oz/2 cups) Greek-style yoghurt

SWEET TOMATO COMPOTE

330 g (11¾ oz/1½ cups) caster
(superfine) sugar

1 cinnamon stick

2 fresh bay leaves

1 tablespoon freshly squeezed lemon juice

1 kg (2 lb 4 oz) roma (plum) tomatoes, halved

METHOD

To make the sweet tomato compote, combine the sugar, cinnamon, bay leaves and lemon juice in a saucepan with 500 ml (17 fl oz/2 cups) water. Slowly bring the mixture to a simmer, stirring to dissolve the sugar. Add the tomato, bring back just to a simmer, then reduce the heat to low and cook for about 50 minutes, or until the liquid has reduced and thickened — place an inverted saucer or small plate over the tomato halves to keep them submerged while cooking. Remove from the heat and cool, discarding the cinnamon.

To make the yoghurt cream, sprinkle the gelatine into a small heatproof cup and add 2½ tablespoons cold water; stand for 5 minutes until softened. Place the cup in a small saucepan of gently simmering water and heat until the gelatine dissolves. Meanwhile, combine the cream and sugar in a saucepan and heat, stirring to dissolve the sugar, until nearly simmering, then remove from the heat. Stir in the gelatine mixture and cool to room temperature. Add the yoghurt and whisk until smooth. Divide the mixture between six 300 ml (10½ fl oz) glasses and refrigerate for 3–4 hours or overnight.

Serve the chilled yoghurt cream with the sweet tomato compote spooned over the top. **SERVES 6**

بسم الله الرحمن الرحيم وبه نستعين

الحمد لله الذي أنعم علينا بنعمته ثم الصالحات وعلى رسله

أزكى السلام وأنمى التحيات والصلوات ...

بعون الله بنا هذه المدرسة الشريفة المباركة ...

الفاضل الأجل الكامل فخر المرسلين ...

الشهير زاده عليه النعمة السعادة أدامه الله وعلى جملة لوجوه الكرم ووقفه والملك الأعظم

ونافع ومن النفع لا من الله في السلم والعلم برد الله في سنة وستمائة وألف

SWEET CHEESE PIE WITH OVEN-POACHED QUINCE

METHOD

To make the oven-poached quince, preheat the oven to 180°C (350°F/Gas 4). Arrange the quince halves in a single layer in a baking dish and scatter over the sugar and cinnamon. Pour over the boiling water, then cover the dish tightly with foil and cook for 45 minutes. Turn the quince over and cook for a further 45–50 minutes, or until the quince halves are tender. Remove from the heat and cool in the syrup. Cut the quince into thin slices to serve, reserving the syrup.

To make the sweet cheese pie, combine the caster sugar and 125 ml (4 fl oz/ ½ cup) water in a saucepan over medium–low heat. Bring to a simmer and cook for 5 minutes, then remove from the heat, add the lemon juice and cool.

Put the ricotta, vanilla seeds, eggs and icing sugar in a food processor and process until smooth and combined. Add the cream and use the pulse button to process until just combined. Add the flour and pulse again until smooth. Set aside.

Brush the base and side of a 24 cm (9½ inch) round baking dish generously with butter. Place a sheet of filo pastry in the base of the dish and brush well with butter (keep the remaining pastry under a damp tea towel (dish towel) to prevent it drying out as you work). Place another layer of pastry over the top at an angle so that half of the sheet overhangs the sides. Brush with butter and continue layering the pastry at varying angles so that the overhang evenly lines the dish. Spoon the ricotta mixture into the pastry-lined dish. Fold the overhanging pastry back over the filling to cover — you can tear off some pieces of leftover pastry, scrunch them up and use them to fill any remaining gaps in the centre. Bake the pie in the oven for 40 minutes, or until golden and slightly puffed. Remove from the oven and spoon the reserved quince syrup over the top, then leave to cool to room temperature. Cut the pastry into slices and serve with the quince on the side. This pie is best served on the day it is made. **SERVES 8**

INGREDIENTS

220 g (7¾ oz/1 cup) caster (superfine) sugar

1 tablespoon freshly squeezed lemon juice

700 g (1 lb 9 oz) firm fresh ricotta cheese

1 vanilla bean, split lengthways, seeds scraped

2 eggs

2½ tablespoons icing (confectioners') sugar

125 ml (4 fl oz/½ cup) pouring (whipping) cream

1½ tablespoons plain (all-purpose) flour, sifted

8 sheets filo pastry

125 g (4½ oz) butter, melted

OVEN-POACHED QUINCE

3 quinces, peeled, cored and halved

330 g (11¾ oz/1½ cups) caster (superfine) sugar

2 cinnamon sticks

625 ml (21½ fl oz/2½ cups) boiling water

KATMER

INGREDIENTS

110 g (3¾ oz/½ cup) caster (superfine) sugar

1 teaspoon dried yeast

300 g (10½ oz/2 cups) plain (all-purpose) flour, sifted

1 teaspoon salt

125 g (4½ oz) pistachios

60 g (2¼ oz) butter, melted

VANILLA CREAM

125 ml (4 fl oz/½ cup) pouring (whipping) cream

125 ml (4 fl oz/½ cup) full-cream (whole) milk

½ vanilla bean, seeds scraped or 1 teaspoon natural vanilla extract

2 egg yolks

60 g (2¼ oz) caster (superfine) sugar

2 tablespoons plain (all-purpose) flour

METHOD

To make the vanilla cream, combine the cream, half the milk and the vanilla seeds, if using, in a small saucepan and bring just to a simmer. Remove from the heat. Meanwhile, combine the egg yolks and sugar in a bowl, then add the remaining milk and the flour, whisking until the mixture is smooth. Pour the hot milk mixture into the egg mixture and return the mixture to a clean saucepan, stirring constantly to prevent lumps forming, bring to the boil. Cook over medium heat, stirring often, for 2 minutes, then remove from the heat. Transfer to a bowl and place a piece of lightly buttered baking paper directly on the surface to prevent a skin forming. Cool to room temperature and stir in the vanilla extract, if using. Vanilla cream can be made up to 2 days in advance and can be stored in an airtight container in the refrigerator.

To make the dough, combine 1 teaspoon of the sugar and 150 ml (5 fl oz) lukewarm water in a small bowl, then sprinkle over the yeast. Set aside for about 8 minutes, or until foamy, then add another 80 ml (2½ fl oz/⅓ cup) lukewarm water. Combine the flour and salt in a bowl, then add the yeast mixture and stir to form a soft dough, adding more water if necessary. Turn out onto a lightly floured surface and knead for 5 minutes, or until the dough is smooth and elastic. Roll the dough into a ball and place in a lightly oiled bowl, turning to coat. Cover with plastic wrap and set aside in a warm, draught-free place for 1 hour, or until doubled in size.

Meanwhile, combine the pistachios and remaining sugar in a food processor then process until a coarse powder forms.

Knock back the dough on a lightly floured surface, then divide the dough into ten even-sized pieces. Working with one piece at a time, roll each out to create a 22 x 20 cm (8½ x 8 inch) rectangle. Take care not to tear the dough — it should be quite thin and needs to be well floured so as to not stick to the work surface. Brush each rectangle of dough with melted butter, then scatter over a scant 2 tablespoons of the pistachio mixture leaving a 2 cm (¾ inch) border around the edges. Place 1 tablespoon of the vanilla cream, in small random dabs, over the nuts. Gently stretch the long sides of the dough over to meet in the middle and press to seal, then fold over the shorter sides to form a rectangular parcel, about 12 x 9 cm (4½ x 3½ inch), pressing to seal

Heat a large, heavy-based frying pan over medium–low heat. Brush the base generously with melted butter and cook the katmer, in batches, for 3–4 minutes on each side, or until deep golden and crisp. Serve hot or warm. **MAKES 10**

This dessert (along with candied green walnuts, candied tomato and candied baby eggplant) is a feature on the menu at the popular Istanbul restaurant Ciya. This recipe is a scaled-back, more user-friendly version — to make it the traditional way requires roasting the pumpkin with calcium hydroxide (or slaked lime).

CANDIED PUMPKIN

INGREDIENTS

440 g (15½ oz/2 cups) caster (superfine) sugar
1.5 kg (3 lb 5 oz) jap pumpkin
    (winter squash), peeled, seeded and
    cut into 5 cm (2 inch) pieces
sesame seeds, to serve
thick (double/heavy) cream, to serve

METHOD

Put the sugar, pumpkin and 125 ml (4 fl oz/½ cup) water in a large saucepan and slowly bring to a simmer. Cover the pan and cook over low heat for 30 minutes, or until the sugar has dissolved and the pumpkin has given up its juices. Remove the lid and simmer gently for about 1½ hours, or until the liquid has reduced and thickened. Remove from the heat and cool the pumpkin in the syrup. The candied pumpkin can be stored in an airtight container in the refrigerator for up to 2 weeks.

Serve the pumpkin at room temperature with sesame seeds sprinkled over and a dollop of cream on the side. **SERVES 6–8**

A CUP OF MIRRA IN MARDIN

I was lured to Mardin by the promise of an atmospheric old-world Arab-flavoured city, full of historically significant Syriac Christian churches and lovely old homes, many of which have striking decorations carved into their stony facades. They're the colour of honeycomb and built into the side of a steep hill, overlooking the Mesopotamian Plain that sweeps on into nearby Syria. Streets are steep and narrow and duties, such as the delivery of goods to the lively food market, are carried out as they have been for centuries, by donkeys.

For most of my stay I dine at the Kamer Vakfi, one of a chain of restaurants established throughout south-eastern Anatolia to help women, often in difficult domestic situations, earn a little money and independence. There's a rotating roster of ten women who take turns to service the menu. If I come early enough I can catch the cook at work, deftly fashioning strips of yufka dough and bits of crumbly cheese into ciğara börek, stuffing köfte ready for frying, or gutting pomegranates.

My other favourite haunt is an antique shop in town where I find myself seriously contemplating a set of old amber-coloured prayer beads, finished at the base with a swag of 1930s Turkish coins. Every time I come to lust after them I'm offered a cup of mirra, coffee so thick it's practically molasses … minus the sweetness. My relationship with this unique coffee style develops rapidly from revulsion to devotion. Known colloquially as *sahos ayiltan* ('that which sobers a drunk') mirra is consumed throughout the south-east where it is associated with festivals and ceremonies such as weddings. I soon find out there is an entire protocol that surrounds its consumption. Mirra is made via an elaborate process involving repeated boiling, cooling and the pouring off of sediment; I am told it can take eight hours and three people to make — one to stir the liquid, one to pour in the coffee and another to sing the ballads. It's made in large quantities and reheated as needed. It is always served in tiny cups without a handle and as a mark of respect older people are served first. It's impolite to refuse a cup, as it takes great effort to make, and once the cup is drained (in one swig is considered proper) it must be handed back to the host, never put down. Mirra takes 'bitter' to a whole new stratosphere and for a caffeine kick, there's nothing like it on the planet. It clearly impairs judgment too because against my better reasoning, I blow my budget and buy the beads. I blame this on the mirra.

APPLE COMPOTE WITH TOASTED SESAME ICE CREAM AND SESAME BISCUITS

INGREDIENTS

750 ml (26 fl oz/3 cups) apple juice

385 g (13½ oz/1¾ cups) caster
    (superfine) sugar

3 English Breakfast tea bags

2 cinnamon sticks

½ teaspoon whole cloves

900 g (2 lb) small granny smith apples,
    peeled and halved

SESAME BISCUITS

260 g (9¼ oz/1¾ cups) plain
    (all-purpose) flour

¾ teaspoon baking powder

125 g (4½ oz) butter, melted

60 ml (2 fl oz/¼ cup) full-cream
    (whole) milk

75 g (2¾ oz/⅓ cup) caster (superfine) sugar

1 teaspoon natural vanilla extract

1 egg yolk

1 teaspoon ground cardamom

1 egg, whisked well

150 g (5½ oz/1 cup) sesame seeds

TOASTED SESAME ICE CREAM

310 ml (10¾ fl oz/1¼ cups) full-cream
    (whole) milk

560 ml (19¼ fl oz/2¼ cups) pouring
    (whipping) cream

6 egg yolks

220 g (7¾ oz/1 cup) caster (superfine) sugar

1½ teaspoons natural vanilla extract

90 g (3¼ oz/⅓ cup) tahini

50 g (1¾ oz/⅓ cup) toasted sesame seeds,
    plus extra, for serving

METHOD

To make the toasted sesame ice cream, combine the milk and cream in a saucepan over medium heat and bring just to a simmer. Using hand-held beaters, whisk the egg yolks and sugar in a bowl until thick and pale, then add the vanilla and mix well to combine. Pour the milk mixture into the yolk mixture and stir with a wooden spoon until well combined. Return the mixture to a clean saucepan over medium–low heat and cook for about 8 minutes, stirring continuously with a wooden spoon until the mixture thickens and coats the back of the spoon. Remove from the heat and cool slightly, stirring occasionally to prevent a skin forming. Stir in the tahini and sesame seeds, then cool the mixture to room temperature. Refrigerate to chill, then transfer to an ice-cream machine and churn according to the manufacturer's instructions. Alternatively, transfer to a shallow metal tray and freeze, whisking every couple of hours until frozen and creamy. Ice cream will keep in an airtight container for up to 1 week.

To make the sesame biscuits, preheat the oven to 170°C (325°F/Gas 3) and line a baking tray with baking paper. Sift the flour and baking powder together into a bowl. In a separate bowl, combine the butter, milk, sugar, vanilla, egg yolk and cardamom and whisk well. Add the flour mixture and stir with a wooden spoon until a dough forms. Take 1 heaped tablespoon of the mixture at a time and use your hands to roll it out on a lightly floured surface to create a 12 cm (4½ inch) log, then cut into even halves. Brush the tops and sides with the beaten egg then dip into the sesame seeds to coat. Transfer to the baking tray and repeat until all of the mixture is used. Bake the biscuits for 30 minutes, or until firm to the touch, then transfer to a wire rack to cool. The biscuits will keep in an airtight container for up to 1 week.

To make the apple compote, put the apple juice, sugar, tea bags, cinnamon and cloves in a saucepan over medium–low heat. Slowly bring to the simmer, stirring to dissolve the sugar, then cook for 5 minutes. Remove from the heat, stand for 5 minutes to allow the tea to infuse, then discard the tea bags. Add the apple halves to the syrup. Place a plate on top to weigh the apples down, then cook over a low heat for 10–12 minutes, or until the apples are just tender. Cool to room temperature.

Serve the apple compote with the toasted sesame ice cream and sesame biscuits passed separately. **SERVES 6**

YEAST PANCAKES WITH RICOTTA CREAM AND HONEY-ROSEWATER SYRUP

METHOD

To make the honey-rosewater syrup, combine the honey with 125 ml (4 fl oz/ $\frac{1}{2}$ cup) water in a saucepan over medium–low heat. Bring to a simmer and cook, without stirring, for 20 minutes, or until reduced and deep golden. Cool slightly and stir in the rosewater. Set aside to cool.

To make the ricotta cream, combine the ricotta and icing sugar in a food processor and process until smooth. Add the cardamom and cream and use the pulse button to process until the mixture is thick — do not overprocess or it may curdle. Transfer to a bowl, cover with plastic wrap, and refrigerate until ready to use.

To make the pancakes, put the sugar in a bowl with 60 ml (2 fl oz/$\frac{1}{4}$ cup) lukewarm water and stir to dissolve, then sprinkle over the yeast. Set aside for about 8 minutes, or until foamy, then add 310 ml (10$\frac{3}{4}$ fl oz/1$\frac{1}{4}$ cups) lukewarm water and mix well.

Meanwhile, sift the flour, baking powder and salt into a large bowl and stir in the semolina and caster sugar. Add the yeast mixture and whisk well until a smooth batter forms, then cover with plastic wrap and set aside at room temperature for 30 minutes, or until slightly bubbly.

Heat a large, heavy-based cast-iron frying pan over medium–low heat. Add a little butter and swirl to coat the base of the pan. Drop heaped tablespoons of the mixture into the pan and cook, in batches, for 3–4 minutes each side, or until risen, light golden and cooked through, adding extra butter to the pan as necessary. Transfer to a plate and cover with a clean tea towel (dish towel) while cooking the remaining pancakes. Serve warm or at room temperature, with the ricotta cream spooned over the top, drizzled with the honey–rosewater syrup and sprinkled with the pistachios. **MAKES ABOUT 22**

INGREDIENTS

1 pinch sugar
1 teaspoon dried yeast
225 g (8 oz/1$\frac{1}{2}$ cups) plain (all-purpose) flour
1 teaspoon baking powder
$\frac{1}{2}$ teaspoon salt
60 g (2$\frac{1}{4}$ oz/$\frac{1}{2}$ cup) fine semolina
2 tablespoons caster (superfine) sugar
butter, for cooking
chopped pistachios, for sprinkling

RICOTTA CREAM

250 g (9 oz/1 cup) firm fresh ricotta cheese
60 g (2$\frac{1}{4}$ oz/$\frac{1}{2}$ cup) icing (confectioners') sugar, sifted
seeds from 6 cardamom pods, crushed
250 ml (9 fl oz/1 cup) pouring (whipping) cream

HONEY-ROSEWATER SYRUP

350 g (12 oz/1 cup) honey
1 teaspoon rosewater

Zerde is a type of rice pudding of which the Turks have a number of variations. Translating as 'yellow' in Persian, zerde is light in texture and fragrant with saffron and rosewater. Zerde is an ancient dish that has been served for centuries and is often associated with special occasions.

ZERDE

INGREDIENTS

$\frac{1}{2}$ teaspoon saffron threads

75 g (2¾ oz/⅓ cup) medium-grain white
   rice, rinsed and drained

30 g (1 oz/¼ cup) cornflour (cornstarch)

275 g (9¾ oz/1¼ cups) caster
   (superfine) sugar

1 tablespoon rosewater

50 g (1¾ oz/⅓ cup) currants

40 g (1½ oz/⅓ cup) chopped pistachios

thick (double/heavy) cream, to serve

METHOD

Put the saffron in a small bowl or cup and add 60 ml (2 fl oz/¼ cup) hot water then set aside for 1–2 hours or until deep orange.

Put the rice and 1.5 litres (52 fl oz/6 cups) water in a saucepan and bring to a simmer. Cover the pan, reduce the heat to very low and cook for 20 minutes, or until the rice is tender. Combine the cornflour in a small bowl with 80 ml (2½ fl oz/⅓ cup) cold water and stir to form a smooth paste. Stir the sugar and saffron mixture into the rice and then add the cornflour mixture, stirring constantly for 3–4 minutes, or until it comes to the boil and thickens. Remove from the heat, stir in the rosewater and cool slightly.

Divide the mixture among six 300 ml (10½ fl oz) glasses, sprinkle over the currants and pistachios, then cool to room temperature. Cover with plastic wrap and refrigerate. Serve the zerde chilled with the cream. Zerde will keep, covered in the refrigerator, for up to 4 days. **SERVES 6**

ROASTED PLUMS WITH PEKMEZ SABAYON

METHOD

Heat the oven to 180°C (350°F/Gas 4). Halve the plums, remove the stones and place, cut side up, in a single layer in a large baking dish. Scatter over the sugar, then roast in the oven for 15–20 minutes, or until softened. Remove from the oven and cool to room temperature.

To make the pekmez sabayon, put 1 litre (35 fl oz/4 cups) water in a saucepan and bring to the boil. Choose a large bowl that will fit snugly inside the saucepan, making sure it does not touch the water. Away from the heat, combine the egg yolks, sugar, pekmez and 60 ml (2 fl oz/$^1/_2$ cup) water in the bowl. Place the bowl over the simmering water and use hand-held electric beaters to whisk continuously over medium heat for 8–10 minutes, or until the mixture has increased in volume and is very thick — it should hold a ribbon briefly when the beaters are lifted; take care to keep whisking the mixture or it will curdle. Remove the bowl to sit over a bowl of cold water and continue to whisk until the mixture is room temperature. Serve the pekmez sabayon spooned over the plums and scatter over the pistachios. Sabayon can be made up to 1 hour in advance.

SERVES 6

INGREDIENTS

1.25 kg (2 lb 12 oz) firm, ripe plums

2$^1/_2$ tablespoons caster (superfine) sugar

chopped pistachios, to serve

PEKMEZ SABAYON

6 egg yolks

100 g (3$^1/_2$ oz) caster (superfine) sugar

125 ml (4 fl oz/$^1/_2$ cup) pekmez (see note page 73)

HAZELNUT MERINGUES WITH ROSE CREAM AND ROASTED STRAWBERRIES

METHOD

To make the roasted strawberries, preheat the oven to 180°C (350°F/Gas 4). Place the strawberries in a single layer in a baking dish. Sprinkle over the sugar and carefully pour over 125 ml (4 fl oz/½ cup) water, then bake for 25 minutes, or until the strawberries are tender and a syrup has formed. Set aside at room temperature.

To make the rose cream. Combine the quark, icing sugar and rosewater in a food processor and process until smooth and combined. Add the cream and use the pulse button to process the mixture until it is thick and smooth. Stir in enough red food colouring to tint the cream pink, if using. Refrigerate until needed.

Preheat the oven to 150°C (300°F/Gas 2). Line two baking trays with baking paper. Process the roasted hazelnuts until very finely ground.

In a separate bowl, use electric beaters to whisk the egg whites until firm peaks form then, whisking constantly, add the sugar 1 tablespoon at a time, making sure that the sugar has dissolved before adding more — the mixture should be very thick and glossy. Gently fold through the hazelnuts.

Drop heaped tablespoonfuls of the meringue mixture onto the prepared trays and flatten slightly. Bake for 20 minutes, or until dry to the touch. Turn the oven off and allow the meringues to cool completely in the oven.

Sandwich the meringues with the rose cream and serve immediately with the roasted strawberries passed separately. Unfilled meringues will keep, stored in an airtight container, for up to 1 week. **MAKES 18**

Note: Quark cheese is a soft, slightly sour curd cheese — it has a milder flavour and richer texture than yoghurt, which makes it perfect for using in desserts. It is available from most speciality grocery stores and delicatessens.

INGREDIENTS

125 g (4½ oz) hazelnuts, roasted and peeled
3 egg whites
150 g (5½ oz/⅔ cup) caster (superfine) sugar

ROSE CREAM

300 g (10½ oz) quark cheese (see note)
2½ tablespoons icing (confectioners') sugar
1 teaspoon rosewater, or to taste
80 ml (2½ fl oz/⅓ cup) pouring (whipping) cream
3–4 drops red food colouring (optional)

ROASTED STRAWBERRIES

800 g (1 lb 12 oz) strawberries, hulled and halved lengthways
220 g (7¾ oz/1 cup) caster (superfine) sugar

POMEGRANATE GEL WITH FAIRY FLOSS

METHOD

Put the pomegranate juice and sugar in a saucepan over medium heat. Bring to a simmer and stir to dissolve the sugar, then continue simmering for 20 minutes, or until nearly reduced by half. Combine the cornflour with just enough water to make a smooth paste and stir until smooth. Add to the pan, stirring constantly, for 3 minutes, or until it boils and thickens. Remove from the heat and cool to room temperature, stirring to prevent a skin forming.

Divide the pomegranate liquid between four or six 200 ml (7 fl oz) capacity serving glasses, then cover each with plastic wrap and refrigerate for 4 hours or overnight to set. Serve the gel in the glasses with the fairy floss piled on top and a scattering of pomegranate seeds. **SERVES 4–6**

Note: Also known as 'pashmak', which means 'little wool' in Persian, this fairy floss originated in Iran, although the Turks have their own version. Persian fairy floss is available from most speciality grocery stores and delicatessens.

INGREDIENTS

1.25 litres (44 fl oz/5 cups) pomegranate juice
145 g (5 oz/^{2}/$_3$ cup) caster (superfine) sugar
40 g (1^1/$_2$ oz/^{1}/$_3$ cup) cornflour (cornstarch)
Persian fairy floss (see note), to serve
pomegranate seeds, to serve

ROSE AND PISTACHIO SWEETMEATS

INGREDIENTS

250 g (9 oz) pistachios

30 g (1 oz/¼ cup) icing (confectioners') sugar

220 g (7¾ oz/1 cup) caster (superfine) sugar

2 tablespoons liquid glucose

3 teaspoons rosewater

pink cachous, to decorate

METHOD

Put the pistachios and icing sugar in a food processor and process until a very fine meal forms.

Put the caster sugar, liquid glucose and 2½ tablespoons water in a small saucepan over medium–low heat and simmer for about 8 minutes, or until the mixture reaches the 'soft ball' stage (this happens when a small amount of the mixture will form a soft, pliable ball when dropped into a glass of cold water). Remove from the heat and, with the motor running, pour the sugar mixture into the food processor with the pistachio mixture, adding the rosewater. Process until the mixture forms a paste, then remove to a large bowl and cool slightly.

When just cool enough to handle (mixture will still be quite hot) use your hands to knead until it is smooth and pliable. Take 1 heaped teaspoonful of the mixture at a time and use your hands to roll into neat balls. While still warm, press a pink cachous into each, then place in paper cases.

Serve the rose and pistachio sweetmeats with tea or coffee. Rose and pistachio sweetmeats can be stored in an airtight container at room temperature for up to 5 days. **MAKES ABOUT 28**

COFFEE CUSTARDS WITH HALVA PASTRIES

METHOD

To make the coffee custards, preheat the oven to 160°C (315°F/Gas 2–3). Put the milk, cream, espresso coffee, cardamom and sugar in a saucepan and stir over medium heat for 3–4 minutes, or until the sugar has dissolved. Remove from the heat and cool slightly. Strain into a large bowl, discarding the cardamom.

Add the egg yolk to the milk mixture and stir to mix well. Divide the mixture among six 250 ml (9 fl oz/1 cup) ovenproof ramekins (dariole moulds) and place them in a large baking dish. Pour in enough boiling water to come halfway up the sides of the ramekins, then bake in the oven for 45 minutes, or until nearly set — the custards should still be slightly wobbly in the centre. Cool to room temperature, then cover with plastic wrap and refrigerate for at least 2 hours, or until chilled.

To make the halva pastries, preheat the oven to 180°C (350°F/Gas 4) and lightly grease a baking tray. Lay a sheet of filo pastry on a clean work surface and brush with melted butter (keep the rest of the pastry under a damp tea towel (dish towel) to prevent them from drying out). Fold in half widthways, then cut in half widthways. Brush each piece with butter then, with the short end facing you, place about 2½ teaspoons of halva along one edge, leaving a 1 cm (½ inch) border on either side. Fold the sides over, then roll the pastry up to form a neat log; do not roll pastries too tight or they will split while baking. Place on the prepared tray and repeat with the remaining filo sheets, butter and halva until all used. Brush the pastries all over with butter, sprinkle with almonds and bake for 15 minutes, or until golden and crisp, then remove to a wire rack and cool. Serve the halva pastries with the chilled coffee custards. **SERVES 6**

Note: Halva is a sweetmeat made from crushed sesame seeds or almonds combined with boiled sugar syrup. It is made in block form and sold in slices, and is available from Middle Eastern and Turkish grocery stores.

INGREDIENTS

250 ml (9 fl oz/1 cup) full-cream (whole) milk

250 ml (9 fl oz/1 cup) pouring (whipping) cream

375 ml (13 fl oz/1½ cups) very strong freshly brewed espresso coffee

4 cardamom pods, bruised

220 g (7¾ oz/1 cup) caster (superfine) sugar

8 egg yolks, lightly beaten

HALVA PASTRIES

6 sheets filo pastry

125 g (4½ oz) butter, melted

175 g (6 oz) halva, crumbled (see note)

40 g (1½ oz/¼ cup) chopped almonds

INDEX

ACKNOWLEDGMENTS

Mist destek na hên lêdan

('You can not clap with one hand') – Kurdish proverb

Many have had a hand in the making of this book, some wittingly and others not so!

Firstly and most importantly, I would like to thank the boys in my life, Andrew and Harry, for so graciously tolerating my extended absences as I prowled around Turkey. To my fabulous photography team — Amanda McLauchlan, Aimee Jones and Anna Shaw — a big *teşekkür ederim*; the book is so beautiful because of your fabulous work. Hugh Ford, Livia Caiazzo and Jacqueline Blanchard, thank you for always being so wonderful to work with and endlessly patient to boot, I salute you!

To all at the team at Murdoch Books, both past and present, I am beyond grateful for your vision and endless encouragement over many years of association: special thanks to Kay Scarlett, Jane Lawson, Vivien Valk, Kylie Walker, Anneka Manning and Juliet Rogers.

Finally I would like to acknowledge the help of numerous others, too many to name, who have assisted this project in myriad ways, from New Zealand to Sydney and all over Turkey — you've variously aided, abetted, advised, supported, fed and cheered me from the sidelines (and made me tea and sold me kilims!) — a heartfelt thanks to you all.

Published in 2011 by Murdoch Books Pty Limited.

Murdoch Books Australia
Pier 8/9
23 Hickson Road
Millers Point NSW 2000
Phone: +61 (0) 2 8220 2000
Fax: +61 (0) 2 8220 2558
www.murdochbooks.com.au

Murdoch Books UK Limited
Erico House, 6th Floor
93–99 Upper Richmond Road
Putney, London SW15 2TG
Phone: +44 (0) 20 8785 5995
Fax: +44 (0) 20 8785 5985
www.murdochbooks.co.uk

Publisher: Kylie Walker
Photographer: Amanda McLauchlan
Stylist: Aimee Jones
Stylist Assistant: Anna Shaw
Designer: Hugh Ford
Project Manager: Livia Caiazzo
Editor: Jacqueline Blanchard
Production Controller: Alexandra Gonzalez

Text copyright © Leanne Kitchen 2011
The moral right of the author has been asserted.
Design copyright © Murdoch Books 2011
Food photography copyright © Amanda McLauchlan 2011
Location photography copyright © Leanne Kitchen 2011

All rights reserved. No part of this publication may be reproduced, stored in a retrieval system or transmitted in any form or by any means, electronic, mechanical, photocopying, recording or otherwise, without the prior written permission of the publisher.

National Library of Australia Cataloguing-in-Publication Data:

Author: Kitchen, Leanne
Title: Turkey: recipes and tales from the road
ISBN: 978-1-74196-599-5 (hbk.)
Notes: Includes index.
Subjects: Cooking, Turkish.
Dewey Number: 641.59561

A catalogue record for this book is available from the British Library.

Printed by 1010 Printing International Limited, China

The publisher thanks Aeria, Bison, Clay & Flax, Little White Dish, Mud Australia, New Direction Imports and Wood Paper Silk for their assistance with the styling of this book.

IMPORTANT: Those who might be at risk from the effects of salmonella poisoning (the elderly, pregnant women, young children and those suffering from immune deficiency diseases) should consult their doctor with any concerns about eating raw eggs.

OVEN GUIDE: You may find cooking times vary depending on the oven you are using. For fan-forced ovens, as a general rule, set the oven temperature to 20°C (35°F) lower than indicated in the recipe.